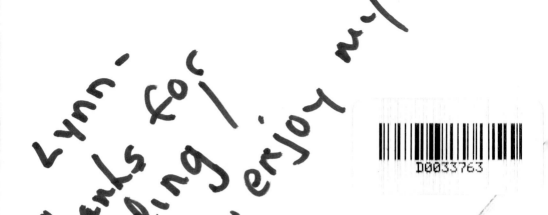

EXECUTIVE HOODLUM

Negotiating on the Corner of Main and Mean

BY JOHN COSTELLO WITH LARRY ELDER

Lynn -
Thanks for
attending !
I hope you enjoy my
book.

This book is for

Mary Patricia McGuinness

Table of Contents

Foreword

It's funny how you think you know someone. I met John about 15 years ago at a Playboy Mansion party and we hit it off right away. He being from Chicago and me from New York we had the same mentality, but we all know New Yorkers are better people. Anyway, we became very good friends. So good that he asked me to be godfather to one of his beautiful young daughters.

Over the years I started to realize how he grew up and who he knew. The stories he told, which I believed to be exaggerated, embellished and any other word you would use to describe someone telling tall tales, were soon made quite real when I met the likes of his sister Margie (Margie, John forced me to mention you; just know I love you and would never want you to be mad at me), Iron Mike RIP, maybe one of the scariest and, amazingly, sweetest humans I have ever met.

After meeting his childhood "buddies" my first thought was to lose his phone number, but cooler heads prevailed and we are still friends. Reading this book I really had no idea how rough his younger years were. The John Costello I know is a good family man, a wonderful father, and a loyal friend.

For him to come from the life he knew as a young man and end up the man he is now is a testament to the intelligence and determination he possesses. It is also a testament to the country we are privileged to live in.

Scott Baio

One

I gave myself a fifty-fifty chance of getting out alive. These were, after all, outfit guys. You've got to understand, in New York they say "wiseguys," but in Chicago it's "outfit guys." Nobody but nobody in Chicago calls himself a wiseguy. It's a dead giveaway that you're from out of town. Technically it was just a "sit-down," meaning a clear-the-air/ sort-things-out meeting with outfit guys I trusted – and who trusted me.

But this was a convince-or-get-killed deal, and I knew it. They did too – no matter the lie they told to guarantee I showed up: "Hey we just wanna talk." But what were my options? Run and keep looking over my shoulder the rest of my life? Maybe my father Mario could do that. Funny that I was named after him. I'm Johnny Costello, Jr., but ever since I was sixteen or seventeen I referred to my father by his stage name. We were never close. I couldn't have called him "dad" or "father" even if he'd wanted me to. You see, my father had, let us say, "misappropriated" 250K in outfit money. That's right – *outfit money*. What kind of outfit guy scams other outfit guys out of a quarter-million dollars? Meet Mario Casini. He scammed the money from a mob-connected bookmaker who had pooled together some outfit guys for

1

my father's "investment opportunity." He'd convinced the bookie that he needed the money to produce a movie about serial killer John Wayne Gacy – and everyone was going to make a bundle of cash! That worked because Gacy was all anybody talked about those days, especially in Chicago where the murders took place. A natural for a movie, right? And somehow, someway and over a long period of time, he convinced the outfit guys that Hollywood wanted *him* to produce it. He said they wanted "realism." Who better to give it to them than a street-smart native Chicagoan who was an outfit associate and knew everybody in town?

One of the people my father knew was Gacy's lawyer – they were friends. A relationship providing him additional credibility. Everybody was well aware that eventually someone would make some kind of a movie about this animal. You wouldn't believe how many streetwise guys fell for my father's scam. He kept telling his outfit "investors" that filming would start as soon as he'd "accumulated enough capital to begin production." That was his classic line. Sounded like he knew what he was talking about. And they'd be "co-producers."

In a word they were hooked – that is until popular Chicago newsman John "Bulldog" Drummond, known for his investigative reporting on Chicago organized crime, unwittingly uncovered the scam. Drummond and well-known journalist Bill Kurtis exposed the story on the local news, focusing on the local businessmen my father took down and going on the assumption that my father was working with the Chicago Outfit on the caper. But neither Drummond nor Kurtis realized the mob had also been victimized by my father. The mob investors knew it only too well. Beaten out of their money, scammed like some clueless "mark." But where was my father? Who knew? Not here. Probably got the hell out of town just in time. And with him gone, so far as the outfit guys were concerned, this left just one question: "Was the kid involved?" Not a chance. Though I'm not sure I myself would have believed I had nothing to do with it. And I'm supposed to convince *them* of that fact. And even if I do succeed in convincing them, who is to say that they won't make an example of me so others don't get bright ideas.

I kept asking myself how in God's name I'd ended up in this position. I was already three years out of college and had started a promising career in the semiconductor industry. Things were going much better than I had expected. Then out of the blue my father calls. I shouldn't have taken the damn call – or at least hung up at the first smell of bullshit. But looking back, I really *wanted* to believe him. My father begged me to "manage his career," as he put it. "C'mon, Yuma, you *know* I can sing" – until I finally conceded that, yeah, yeah, he could sing. And why the name "Yuma"? In the '60s there was an old TV series about a bounty hunter named Johnny Yuma. I was fascinated by the show. So my family started calling me Yuma. When my father really wanted something, wanted to be nice, that's what he called me – Yuma. Perhaps trying to revive some long-lost emotional bond that he imagined had existed but never actually had. Interestingly, the guy who starred in the series, Nick Adams, committed suicide when young. Now it was my turn – because that's what it felt like heading for this sit-down – suicide. But not by choice.

My father had done it again.

How ironic that the sit-down is in my father's restaurant, Mario's Place, right off Roosevelt Road. This had become a hangout for his outfit friends. Mario never made them pay. He instructed the waiters, "I never want to see you bring them a check. You hear me? Never."

It was an old-school place, red leather booths, checkered

table cloths, ambient lighting and pictures of Italian boxers and tenors on the walls. Every weekend there'd be some hardcore outfit guys having a meal or drinking at the bar. Sometimes I'd be there with a date and one of these ruffians would shout across the restaurant: "Johnny, vene qua, vene qua! (c'mere, c'mere) Sit down! Have a seat!" If there was someone at the table whom I didn't know, they would introduce me as "Mario's kid that graduated college." Then I would introduce my date. One was a highly educated girl, not at all accustomed to this atmosphere. After we'd been "called over" and pleasantries exchanged, Eddie Caruso blurted out: "Johnny, I gotta say, every time I see ya in dis joint, you're wit a good lookin' broad." She was terrified, looked as if she had just met Al Capone. He laughed so hard that it made me laugh too. Before we even got back to our table, she asked me to take her home, adding: "Who ARE these people?" Granted, not the best place to take a first date who wasn't from the neighborhood, and I never did *that* again.

For almost a year now my father had owned Mario's Place. Sort of. He'd actually only made a down payment with some of the "movie" money which he stole from the outfit guys and which is why I was heading back there now to begin with.

It's past midnight when I arrive at the restaurant. Now closed to customers, the outfit guys are already there and they let me in through the front door. "Sit in the back," they say and I'm directed to a booth near the kitchen, away from the windows. As I slide in, Eddie Caruso sits directly across from me and his brother Joey climbs in on my side of the booth to wedge me tight against the wall. I'm boxed in. Eddie's in his early fifties, six-foot-two, probably 240 pounds, with a big jaw and thick salt-and-pepper hair. His raspy voice makes him even more scary. Joey is a couple years older, shorter, and has a beer-belly. His complexion is dark like his brother's. But why is Joey even at this sit-down? He's not nearly as involved in the outfit world the way Eddie is. Joey, based on past conversations I've had with him, seems more truculent than Eddie. I've also heard stories. A lot of people confirm that his reputation as a hothead is well deserved.

Who knew when my father bought the place that his son would be offed while sitting in one of his favorite booths? What's more, he'd bought it from the nephew of "Joey the Clown" Lombardo, who was one of the most feared outfit guys in Chicago. And sitting in a chair slightly behind the booth is a guy who with his prematurely white hair looks like the comic Steve Martin – but Ronnie Ross is nobody's comedian. I've known Ronnie a long time and have asked him to come to the meeting. I trust him and feel comfortable around him because he and my father are good friends. I'd hoped that Ronnie might have some influence because I'd heard he was "connected" with Joseph Aiuppa, aka "Joey Doves" and allegedly a high-ranking member of the Chicago Outfit. Ronnie would insist to me that he was completely innocent of any wrongdoing and that I should discount the rumors I'd heard on the street. He was almost incredulous about it, but nonetheless he admitted to being a suspect in over half a dozen homicides. That they let Ronnie come to the sit-down is probably good news. Hard to say. He has no beefs with this crew and therefore nothing to fear – but then again, for all I know, he may have been working with them from the beginning.

After taking my seat I notice a couple others I know or have at least seen before, namely two guys standing in front of the restaurant. What did they think I was going to do – try and run away? One guy out front is Tony Centracchio, impeccably dressed as always. I've met Tony a couple of times in social settings and he always seemed very personable – on another occasion, in my father's office in Park Ridge, not so much. He was obviously riled as he walked briskly past me and the receptionist as if we were invisible and yanked open the door to my father's office. Apparently the night before my father had been at a country club in Oak Brook with Johnny Unger, who was somehow associated with the late Sam Giancana. At another table was Jack Cerrone, the supposed Chicago mob boss at the time, and Johnny allegedly said something way out of line to one of Jack's associates at the table, purportedly Dominic Blasi, previous driver and friend of Sam Giancana. Now Tony was furious and told my old man that he needed to make sure Johnny Unger kept his mouth shut. Then Tony left as fast as he'd come in.

The other guy at the front of the restaurant was someone I'd heard tell of but never been introduced to. I recognized him because of his hat, the type they wear in mob movies. They called him "The Undertaker" because he supposedly buried mob hits in a cemetery.

Eddie Caruso is probably the man accountable to his superiors for my father's actions. I figure he's in charge of this sit-down but can't be exactly sure owing to the presence of Tony Centracchio.

Everybody has an Eddie story. Whenever he got pinched, he managed to walk. Like my father, nothing stuck. One time he allegedly robbed a Robert Hall clothing store, was caught, even convicted by a jury, but ended up walking. His lawyer argued that police set up an improper lineup by having Eddie stand next to a bunch of people that – according to his lawyer – looked nothing like him. And the court of appeals bought it. Most people said it was his lawyer, that he'd bought off some people, but whatever it was, Eddie had succeeded in walking again. In fact Eddie's case became known for "improper police lineup." Eddie was low-key about the whole thing and talked about it with the skill of a defense attorney, saying things like, "I established legal precedent." At first I didn't believe him. So I looked it up – and discovered that it had gone down exactly the way he told it. Then later I met a big-time criminal lawyer who told me he'd studied the "People versus Caruso case" in law school.

Hell, if he kills me tonight, they'll probably throw him in a lineup with a bunch of black dwarves and he walks again.

This is the guy who's deciding my fate.

So Eddie starts in: "Where's the fucking money?"

I take a deep breath, straighten my tie. Coming from college and then to corporate America I always wore suits to meetings. I want these guys to believe I'm professional and honest, that I'm not afraid and have nothing to hide. Who wears a nice expensive suit if he knows it's going to be splattered with his own blood? Not that you're going to need the suit afterward. But I want to project confidence. Trying to keep my voice calm and even, not speaking too fast, I say: "Hey look at how my father lives, look at his house, his cars – even this restaurant. You both saw me arguing with him about his flashy spending and you all laughed your heads off. Remember?"

My eyes move back and forth, looking directly at each of them, never looking down, never hesitating. "Look at how I live. The only fancy place I eat at is here. I got the bank-account registers. I can show you where everything went. I've been living on the money I saved the last three years working after I graduated from college. I had a real job in the semiconductor industry before I came back here to manage my father's career. In short I didn't need this aggravation."

Eddie says: "What about everybody else?"

7

He means all the others my father has brought into the scheme.

"This guy does that, that guy does this, these guys over here I don't know what they did," I reply, speaking the truth. "I can tell you one thing about your money, though, I didn't take it. My father took it. And you know it. You're the ones who gave it to him. I didn't tell you to give him the money!" By now I'm showing indignation, having abandoned the studied approach, and using my hands for emphasis: "You want records, I can give you the records!"

Eddie and Joey look at each other. They slowly get up and walk to the front of the restaurant and stand talking to Tony Centracchio and the Undertaker. It seems like forever. Ronnie is hard to read and looks more serious than I've seen him in the past.

It crosses my mind that Ronnie may be the guy to shoot me in the back of the head if things go sideways. I'm thinking about the scene in *The Godfather* when Michael Corleone goes into the bathroom of an Italian restaurant to retrieve a hidden gun then comes back to kill Solozzo and McCluskey. If Ronnie excuses himself to go to the bathroom, I may have a heart attack! Maybe it's not even Eddie who'll make the call. Ronnie looks like he knows what I'm thinking. He raises his hands, palms upward, as if to say, *Whaddaya want from me? I don't know nuttin.*

No, this is Eddie's call, just as I'd initially thought, and I see three possible outcomes – all bad.

One: *We kill him because we think he was in on it.*

Two: *We kill him to make an example. $250,000 is too much money to let anyone slide – even if he had nothing to do with it.*

Three: *We break his legs as a message to his father so he can imagine what will happen to* **him**.

Oh yes, and a fourth possibility: *Let him go, make him bring his father to us, then kill 'em both.*

I'm thinking, okay, 24 years old and I'm done. Whatever option, one through four, I'm fucking done.

Eddie finally comes back, sits down, close enough to me so I can smell his last drink. "Johnny," he says, "thanks for coming. You're off the hook. I just need you to get some records for me at the office. I can't guarantee anything about your father, but you're off the hook."

I feel like a defendant in a death-penalty trial where the jury returns a verdict of Not Guilty – but with the big difference that if the verdict's guilty then the sentence is immediate – and with no appeals!

I get up. As I start to walk out, Eddie grabs my arm. Shit! Did he change his mind? "Get me the records," he says.

I had dodged a bullet. But from that moment on I became an even harder person than I was before. And I'd never been angrier with my father. A new line had been crossed. He had thrown me to the wolves. I wanted to tell Eddie: *I'll help you find him and kill him myself!* But it was my fault – and I knew it. Given all that I had learned about my father, the things he did, the scams he pulled, I had STILL made the choice to get involved. I'd screwed up royally – namely I'd trusted him.

And my father? He skated too. I kid you not. After all the crap he'd pulled, the guy skated. The money was never repaid nor any settlement reached. I'll never really know why – or which outfit guy made the call. I heard some rumors from some New York guys that John Gotti had interceded on my father's behalf, but I can't confirm this. What I can tell you is that much later, when my father had to appear in Florida for probation-violation hearings, he sang for some of the New York crews at several underground Italian "social clubs."

The only thing I can say for certain is outfit guys and wiseguys loved to hear my father sing. No matter what guy he beat out of his money, his victim didn't want to be the one to silence my father's vocal gift. He was as crooked as they come and never paid any tribute to any boss out of all his scams – nothing – not even a "taste." Strangely enough, after this sit-down not only did Eddie and I become friends but he grew close to my father as well. That was the charm he had. He even teased Eddie about getting taken! He'd give him a smirk and say what he always said to all the "marks," including me, whom he took down: "Did you learn anything?"

Eddie became something of a father figure to me. He mentored me on the Chicago mob hierarchy. He taught me how to read people like a poker player. How to read gestures, how to size them up, how to gauge their true intentions. He counseled me on what to say to get precisely the reaction I sought. How to speak on the phone in a threatening way to get your message across without actually being threatening. He told me things about surviving the Chicago streets that almost nobody knew – for instance who had what political connections and who was on the take. But what Eddie Caruso mostly did for me was confirm that life was survival of the fittest.

"You know the Serengeti, Johnny?"

"Sure, that big ecosystem in Africa."

"Eco-what? You fuckin college kid. I'm talkin' that place with all those animals running around. And you got two types – the predators and the prey – and you gotta ask yourself which you wanna be – a fuckin lion or some sorry-ass wildebeest."

"How about the Great White Hunter who kills them both and mounts their heads on his wall."

"Now you're gettin' the idea."

My father sure as hell had gotten the idea – and his scam had almost gotten *me* killed. It had taken me until the night of the sit-down to see that he was willing to sacrifice his son's very life in order to save himself. This sit-down confirmed what I had believed about him since I was a kid – that I was expendable. To get his hands on money he didn't care whom he hurt or how badly, whom he left exposed or how vulnerable he rendered them. Outfit guy or civilian. Best friend or family. He felt he could always talk his way out of it, charm his way out of it or sing his way out of it – which is exactly what he had done this last time. Let some other poor sucker clean up the mess.

Two

Evolution of the Crime Gene

My father used to tell people he made his living as a roofer, which was true as far as it went, and he was a good roofer too, but that was real work and so the bulk of his income came from singing and hustling. Mostly hustling. It was the one thing that made him truly happy. He loved the game. To him there was no greater kick than a well-earned illegitimate buck. One time he even combined the singing and the roofing and the con – in this case Sammy Cahn the legendary songwriter. When my father moved to California in the early 1970s he took some singing jobs and through his musicians found out where Cahn lived. My father goes to his house and rings the bell and Cahn opens the door. "Your roof needs to be done," he says, and Cahn says, "What are you going to charge me?" My father replies, "Nothing – I just want you to hear me sing." They hit it off pretty well and Sammy Cahn even made a direct call to Johnny Carson on my father's behalf and told him the story. But Carson was in a particularly bad mood and shot down the request for my father to appear on the Tonight Show. Later Sammy asked my father to come and sing at something he was doing, so my father says yeah he'll be there. Well, he didn't come through. Cahn was boiling mad but the next week he asked him again to come and sing and my father said sure. Still a no-show. About a decade later in the 1980s all was forgiven. Cahn appeared on my father's cable show "Mario's Place" and told the story of the "singing roofer" – which I had always thought was bullshit until I saw Sammy Cahn telling the story himself and why I'm telling it now.

My old man was poorly educated, he was expelled from Saint Gregory's High School in tenth grade, but God could he sing. The man was just blessed. He learned music on his own, holing up in his parents' third-floor attic and listening to Mario Lanza and Enrico Caruso records on an old Victrola, singing along in an attempt to replicate the notes. While kids his age rocked to Elvis and Fats Domino, he was warbling Verdi and Puccini. He sang with the windows flung open and neighbors could hear him blocks away. Many came out or sat by their windows to listen. It was like a free concert three or four times a week. And he was just sixteen or seventeen at the time. He sang in perfectly accented Italian, though he never learned the language, and not a single voice lesson. But in the same measure as he was blessed with this incredible vocal talent, he was also cursed with a cunning and devious criminal mind. The natural career path of regularly performing and building a fan base? Nah, that's work. What chumps do. Con artists separate "marks" from their money, exceptional con artists often get that mark to come back for more, and my father was beyond exceptional since they almost *always* seemed to come back. Even when the victim wised up, it was difficult if not impossible for him to exact retribution since my father was not only a tough guy but a tough guy with serious connections. And on top of that, as already indicated, he was charismatic. People trusted him. Or wanted to. They got suckered – or suckered themselves – into believing everything he told them no matter how bold or outrageous his claims – and when things went south he could convince them that, really, it was just a matter of time before everything would be fine.

The process was nearly foolproof. He'd invite people to see him perform at a local opera, show or nightclub. He told each of them that he or she was his personal guest, even acknowledging their presence by name during the performance. Captivated by his voice, they were ready to be taken down. Inviting them backstage he would tell them, in all confidence, about a movie project that was "in development" and needed just one or two more "investors." Or maybe it was a record album just short of the money needed to meet its release date. Whatever. Hook, line and sinker.

Hey I'm recording an album, making a movie on Mario Lanza, another one on John Gacy, got a deal with Paramount, we're gonna do this, we're gonna do that . . .

Just fill in the blanks. The details were solely dependent on his mood or what hustle he thought would work on whom. Then out came the wallets, purses and checkbooks.

Once he got the money he would a) never start the project, or b) do the absolute minimum to make it appear that the project was real. Perfect example. In the late '70s and early '80s he was four-walling in Vegas at the Dunes, which means he was keeping all the ticket receipts instead of splitting them with management, which got its cut from the gambling and liquor revenue. (This was a common arrangement in those days, so not one of his scams – for a change.) Renowned comedians Milton Berle, Jackie Vernon, Jack Carter, Pat Cooper and others were his opening act, some of the same guys who opened for Frank Sinatra and Dean Martin; then the comedian would be followed by a female singer/performer, usually one from the Mario Lanza era like Katherine Grayson; and then Mario Casini was on. The local papers or trades would cover the show, my father typically getting rave reviews, and the audiences only got bigger. When the marks came backstage he might whip out a couple of "movie scripts in the works" and they'd proceed to "invest" in the phantom projects. This was particularly effective with someone who had *already* been taken. Don't ask me how that worked, I'm not smart enough to penetrate the mind of a gullible mark, though maybe they were just trying to recoup their losses.

But in an attempt to figure out where my father inherited his crime gene, I did some research into my family history. It was my great-grandfather Beniamino Gagliardi who originally made the long voyage from Sicily to America. Apart from a short stay in a Sicilian juvenile detention center at the age of thirteen, in America he would seem to have been an upstanding citizen, even in 1910 helping to found the "Sons of Italy" Il Sole lodge #52. Beniamino's son Oswaldo may have been a different story. It's hard to separate fact from fiction, but some claim he had gone back to Italy at one point and then returned to America around 1917 under, as one relative put it, "stressful circumstances." Word was that in Italy he had killed someone, was on the run, and re-entered the U.S. through the Canadian backdoor. When I was very young I once asked him why he had left Sicily for the U.S. and he said he was in "bad trouble" but gave no details. I also have an aunt who swears that my grandfather was a prison inmate in Terre Haute, Indiana, on a charge of counterfeiting. In any event, at latest by 1940, he had officially changed his name to "John Costello." The assumed name of a man leaving behind a turbulent past? Anyway I'm the bearer of it. The name I mean, and maybe the other part too.

By the late 1940s my grandfather was owner of a Chicago tavern on Montrose and Western called The Black Cat. There was a neighborhood rumor that he killed someone in the alley outside his bar – or let's put it this way: someone found the body of a guy there that my grandfather didn't like. It seems my grandfather had repeatedly warned the victim to stay away from his bar and the man had refused to comply and one day he ended up dead. My grandfather was never charged. And from then on he appears to have straightened up. He was prudent, saved his money and later bought an apartment building. This was followed by further purchases of investment properties. Some family members said he kept these properties in tip-top shape. Others describe him as a slumlord. In any case he was successful and made good money, epitomizing the "American Dream," an immigrant who found eventual success in the Chicago real-estate market through industry and perseverance. Unfortunately my father had no such work ethic. My grandfather encouraged him to emulate his business model by gifting him with one of his buildings. An opportunity most sane people would have jumped at. But instead of embracing my grandfather's generosity and guidance, my father wanted no part of it because of the work entailed. This was good money but not easy money and of no interest to someone with my father's mindset.

He was born in 1938 and also christened with the name John Costello. He grew up on the streets of Chicago's north side, knew all the local hoods, and ran with a gang called the Shamrocks. Not only had he been smoking cigarettes practically straight from the crib but he loved to fight, which was the reason why he got expelled from school in the tenth grade. He couldn't have cared less. In his view, school was a complete waste of time. There was too much easy money to be made on the streets. His first "job" was shaking down a bookie – which led to the first of many close calls that nearly killed my father. There are many rumors surrounding the 1955 bombing incident on Lakewood and Catalpa in

North Chicago, but the most believable account came from an old-time outfit guy who knew my father. Tired of being fleeced by a reckless punk, the bookie decided to finally take my father out with a car bomb. Unfortunately for the bookie, while approaching the car with bomb in hand, he tripped over a lawn barrier and blew both the car and himself to pieces. The intended victim, presumably my father, was the first to find the body of his would-be assassin. Or at least most of it. Cops found other body parts nearly a block away. Since the bookie had been involved in the "bootleggers war" in Iowa where Louis "Cockeyed" Fratto lived, and Fratto had worked for Al Capone, nobody knows for sure the planned target. But it was my father's car that was destroyed and both he and my grandfather were later questioned by police. No one was arrested for this crime – which was typical of 1950s Chicago when dozens if not hundreds of car bombs detonated throughout the city and few if any people were ever brought to account.

I always referred to my father by one of his aliases – "Mario" as in Mario Casini or "Gianni" as in Gianni Costa – but his sister, my Aunt Karen, always kept to calling him "Johnny." She told me: "You could never ever in your life meet somebody like Johnny. He's like someone that somebody made up." There were also two brothers – both worked construction, mostly roofing, which was how my father acquired the trade – but his four sisters were every bit as rough, if not rougher, than the brothers. They were so scary that their husbands learned to sleep with one eye open whenever they felt that the sisters suspected them of cheating. In a lot of households it was customary to cheat on your wife – though hardly advisable with my aunts. For instance, we called my Aunt Linda the "Merry Widow." Her first husband was shot to death; the next husband, the guy who'd killed her first husband, was the one that cops initially accused my father of killing (he was mysteriously hit by a truck); and then her third husband had died – granted after she broke up with him but still before they were officially divorced – of a drug overdose. We used to tease Aunt Linda that the minute she started dating somebody, the undertaker would come and start measuring the poor sap. My aunts were all pretty crazy, and Karen was the most normal of the bunch, but that's like being considered the sanest person in a loony bin. In any case she was eight years younger than Johnny and used to sell pictures of her handsome brother for five cents a photo to the other girls in her grade school. "I made a lot of money." One day he was sitting there with some lady – she was maybe forty years older than him. I asked him what he was doing with this ugly broad. He just looked at me, laughed, and after he leaned over and kissed the woman he showed me a check made out to him for $10,000! He had a flock just a little smaller than Jesus Christ. All the kids in the neighborhood admired Johnny. Hell, so did most of the men. No matter what he did, how many crooked stunts he pulled, how many people he deceived, how many people he cheated out of money, nobody ever got mad at him – at least not for very long. They felt they had nothing to forgive him for. They thought *he* was right and that *they* should have known better. He could've been anything – a movie star, an evangelist, a dictator, anything. He was that charismatic. People were drawn to him like a junkie is drawn to heroin."

He had lots of girlfriends and there were plenty of rumors about out-of-wedlock kids. But one thing's for certain – when he was nineteen he fell in love. With the woman who was to become my mother. Her name was Patricia, she was also still a teenager, and it must have been love because when they got married he still hadn't knocked her up – their daughter

Margie, my older sister, came only a year and a half later.

My mother herself was the daughter of a Chicago beat cop and she was very Catholic, very gentle, quite lovely, with long black hair, and when she walked down the street she didn't turn men's heads. She broke their necks. So she had that in common with my father, otherwise nothing else. Particularly the fact that she was the offspring of law enforcement. It wasn't long after the nuptials that signs of physical abuse began to appear. She always gave her father excuses about the bruises and other marks on her body, and later those which could be seen on her own knuckles, for pretty soon she started hitting my father back when he was drunk or angry and lashed out. Not that her father or her sisters believed her excuses. But she never asked her father to intervene. She would deal with this on her own.

My mother's parents were predominantly blue-collar people, of Irish descent, and both born and raised in Chicago. My grandfather John McGuinness, affectionately called "Grandpa Mac," was born in 1912 to parents from Castlebar, Ireland, and whose respective families were landowners with a history of holding politically related jobs. Grandpa Mac's three brothers Richard, Mike and Jimmy all went to St. George Catholic High School in Chicago, and after the war John and Richard joined the Chicago Police Department. Mike ended up working for AT&T. I'm uncertain of Jimmy's fate but know he was a bit off mentally. I would periodically see him walking the streets of our neighborhood mumbling to himself. Grandpa Mac was a street cop for twenty-three years then worked for the Chicago Park District another nineteen. His brother Richard remained a cop and was promoted to District Commander of Chicago's 20th District on Foster Avenue.

I loved listening to my grandfather's stories about patrolling the streets of postwar Chicago. He told me how he initially wanted to be a good cop and not accept bribes, which were commonplace, and he was embarrassed by some of his other admissions, but I found them interesting and consistent with what I had witnessed first-hand. After all, by the time I was in my early twenties I had paid off two cops for minor crap. Once for parking too long at the airport, the other to avoid a speeding ticket on the Kennedy Expressway. In those days the Chicago Police patrolled the tollways. As I recall, this duty was eventually assumed by the Illinois State Troopers – probably because the cops were making all the money on ticket revenue and denying it to the state.

My grandmother, who in my eyes was a saint, was Irish as well but her ancestors had long been in the United States. She spoke little about her family history to her kids and even less to us grandkids. She was a soft-spoken, patient and caring person – the exact opposite of my paternal grandmother. Throughout the years, as I grew into adulthood and whenever I visited Chicago, I made a point of taking her to lunch or breakfast. My grandmother never had anything disparaging to say about anyone, though once in a while others on my mom's side of the family would say something derogatory, either subtly or unsubtly, about my father or the Costellos in general, and of course it would be absolutely true. I shrugged it off because I was used to such comments – I'd been hearing them since I was ten or eleven years old. Nevertheless I *was* a Costello, so it still made me feel like an outsider. In my not-yet-mature mind I thought that because I had the exact same name as my father, my presence was a constant reminder to the McGuinness clan of his various misdeeds. And even though I had many good times with my aunts, uncles and cousins on my mother's side of the family, I kept them at arm's length emotionally. And with few exceptions I did the same with my father's side of the family, but of course for slightly different reasons.

Like my father, my mother was born in Chicago in 1938. Her given name was Mary Patricia McGuinness but she preferred to be called "Pat" instead of "Mary Pat." My mom's younger sister was very fond of her, and it has only been in recent years that I've been able to discuss these sensitive matters with Aunt Carol, whose reminiscing brought back to me the many pleasant childhood memories which had been obscured and overshadowed by the bad ones for so long. But Carol had always spoken of her "wonderful sister," three years older than herself, "beautiful, smart, nice," and one day she told me a story I didn't know – how her happy-go-lucky father, my Grandpa Mac, the night before the wedding, came into the kitchen with the family gathered around the table, all the women in curlers, and handed Pat an envelope filled with $1500 in cash and begged her: "Just take this money, go somewhere, don't do it." Maybe that's why, when her husband later slapped her around or was otherwise out of line, she never went running to daddy – she didn't want to give him the satisfaction of saying *I told you so . . .*

Three

THE TURMOIL BEGINS

I was born in 1961 in St. Joseph's Hospital on Chicago's Lakeshore Drive – "born on LSD" as people in my neighborhood used to say. Maybe that wouldn't have been such a bad notion, might have made my childhood easier. But there's a few nice things I remember. I recall the two-flat apartment on Oakley Avenue on Chicago's north side with the electric trolley cars going by and the sky outside crisscrossed with wires. The two-flat was owned by my grandfather whom we called "Papa," so its other floor was occupied by my Aunt Arlene along with her kids. It was great having a close-knit family around all the time, and on Sundays the whole Costello clan gathered for a traditional Italian feast. This was an all-day event and when we left we were always extremely full and very tired. I would play catch with my cousins while the adults were inside, the men drinking beer and discussing sports or local politics while the women helped in the kitchen. After stuffing our faces with great Italian food we scrammed for the basement to play with toys while my uncles and grandfather played small-stakes poker. My grandfather had a foolproof method of winning – namely he cheated – and I was his accomplice. He would call me over, whisper in my ear what others thought was just doting-grandpa talk, but he was actually telling me to covertly look at my father's and uncles' cards. After I'd had my peek he would say: "Johnny, come here and give your Papa a hug!" I would then whisper in his ear who had what cards. It was a good system.

And that's about all I remember of Chicago – at least the stuff I remember fondly.

When I was about six or seven my father moved out to California to pursue his singing career. For all practical purposes my parents had separated, but still the plan was that we'd follow him out to the west coast. I'm not sure of the reasoning behind that. All I remember is my mom saying that we were "his responsibility." Anyway, while waiting for him to send for us, our family lived in my mother's parents' basement, which Grandpa Mac had converted into an apartment. I'm not certain how long we lived there, but hearing the adults talk I knew my father was in no hurry to fly us out.

My father's violent sisters were very resistant to us moving to California – for all I know, he may have encouraged them to threaten my mother not to follow him. One of the most vivid memories I have as a kid, when I was around eight or nine years old, and just before we moved to California, was in the two-flat on North Oakley. I heard screaming and went outside and saw two of my father's sisters beating my mother up on the front porch, one pulling her hair and the other kicking her. I started yelling at them to stop, but it was a helpless feeling.

When we finally did get the call from my father to move to California, sometime in 1969 or 1970, my mother's parents and sisters tried to talk her out of it. But she was probably thinking of the nice home and about getting away from all the Costello people, and maybe my father had been away long enough that she'd forgotten just what a self-serving jerk he could be. I really can't say what she was thinking. But her sister, my Aunt Carol, later told me that when we all went to the airport my Grandpa Mac was carrying his gun. He always carried it, but this time he was ready to blow someone's brains out if they came near us, since there had been threats from my father's side of the family if my mother moved to California. But we got on the plane without incident and a few hours later had touched down in Los Angeles.

For several days we stayed in a hotel until moving to a small apartment in North Hollywood where I had a ringside seat at one of my father's fights. He was not a physically imposing man, but well-muscled and a skilled street fighter who didn't care how big or strong the adversary. It was a weekend morning and we were heading out to breakfast. My father was blasting his opera music while getting ready to leave and sang along with the tenor he was studying – such a precise rendering that it was hard to tell the two apart. The apartment-dweller above us was apparently not an opera lover and came storming down and banged on our door. My father opened the door to an angry tirade from our sizeable neighbor and without hesitation drilled him on the chin so hard that he fell forward into our doorway and lay motionless. Knocked out cold. My father calmly dragged him by his feet, face down, and left him outside just a few feet from the door and resumed singing. Minutes later we all exited the apartment, stepping over our still unconscious neighbor, and headed to the restaurant.

As can be imagined, we moved around a lot those first years, living in Sherman Oaks, in Reseda and two different houses in Woodland Hills. Transferring schools and neighborhood-hopping the whole time made it difficult to make friends. My father only came around once in a while, maybe two or three times a week and sometimes on weekends.

I was too young to understand where he was and what he was doing, but I had my mother. I always went out of my way to please her. I received good grades and was very conscientious about doing my homework right away when I came home from school – unlike my brother and sister who hated school. At night I used to sit at the base of the couch and watch TV with my mother who would be on the couch and twirling the hair on the back of my head.

"Johnny,that was a nice report card you brought home today, almost straight A's. If you keep that up, you're off to college someday."

"Is college nice?"

"It's a great opportunity – I wish I'd been."

"Why didn't you?"

"I married your father."

"You shoulda went to college."

"I should have *gone* to college. But then you wouldn't be here today. I wouldn't have liked that."

"I'm only going if you come with."

"What about Daddy?"

"I don't care about him."

"Oh Johnny, don't talk that way."

Then on 17 May 1971, shortly before my tenth birthday, my life took a dramatic turn. Although my father wasn't often to be seen those days, he still made his presence felt by trying to control my mother and became insanely jealous if he thought she was consorting with other men. One night he followed her back from a bowling alley not far from our house on Penfield Avenue in Woodland Hills. Since my bedroom faced the street I could hear the commotion. I tried to ignore it but couldn't. I got up and looked through the window and saw my parents screaming at each other. Nothing new there. But I must have blocked out the rest – because that night my father beat my mother mercilessly. She was taken by ambulance to Northridge Hospital and was still unconscious when admitted to intensive care. The official police report said that she had a ruptured spleen along with multiple contusions on her head, face, chest, abdomen, legs and arms – everywhere but her back. So she'd put up a fight.[1]

The next morning I arose not sensing anything wrong. I don't recall who was at the house or any communication I might have had with them. I know I walked to Calvert Elementary School and started my day like any other. A couple hours into school a man in a suit walked into the classroom and spoke briefly to my teacher Mrs. Gallup. The moment he entered I knew he was there for me. The teacher told me to collect my belongings and go with the man, and as I gathered my things and walked to the front of the class, all the kids staring at me, I realized that I hadn't seen my mother before leaving the house that morning.

As I entered the car with this stranger, I noticed it was one of those unmarked police cars (my father had schooled me how to spot one – American make, very clean, no hubcaps, and a spotlight on the side window). I began to feel uneasy and had little to say as the detective attempted to make small talk. I stuck to one-word replies. I was afraid to ask any questions myself because I feared the answers I might receive. I just sat there and stared out the window and wondered what would happen next. After about a fifteen or twenty-minute drive, the detective brought me into an office building with harsh strip lights and steel desks.

There were no other cops or police cars in the parking lot so I knew immediately this was not a police station. The man handed me off to a woman and said that she would take care

---

[1] I did not read the police report until many years afterward. Grandpa Mac had given it to me in a sealed envelope in my mid-twenties, which I didn't open until some two decades later. It held no surprises.

of me. I had little dialogue with this woman since I continued to clam up, in part to hold my emotion in check. It seemed I was in that place for hours and those glaring lights gave me a nasty headache.

But then finally the woman led me outside and into a car and we drove a short distance to a kind of rundown neighborhood. The yards were poorly kept and there was lots of dead grass and dirt. We stopped at one of these houses and walked to the front door where we were met by a woman in an apron who was older than my mom and not very pretty. She invited us in and we had a seat in the living room, which had a dull yellow carpet with stains all over it. While the two women talked, a couple blond-haired kids wandered in, one sucking his thumb, and sat next to the woman in the apron and just stared at me with unblinking blue eyes. Or maybe they weren't blue. But they might as well have been in comparison to me with my dark brown ones, black hair and olive skin, which made me feel like an alien race. Then the social worker, or whatever she was, turned to me and said: "This is going to be your new home and family." I was shocked. I wanted to blurt out *Says who!* – but again I kept my mouth shut and tried to gather my thoughts. This must be a foster home. I knew foster homes from watching TV programs. Foster homes were for kids whose parents had died – or didn't want them. Later that evening, after the social worker had left, the rest of the family materialized – a father and three older boys, all blond, all very friendly, overly friendly, with the tone of voice people used when playing with a new puppy. I put on my best face and tried being friendly in turn, but my first day there was a nightmare as I listened to all the long-term plans they had for me. I couldn't fathom the thought of never returning home and seeing my family again, and as they spoke I just stared blindly at their mouths and tuned them out and kept thinking:

No way I'm joining the Cub Scouts, and I'd rather slit my wrists than take music lessons or stay here another day! How about you and Mr. Sunshine over there start by telling me what happened to my mother, brother and sister? That's what I wanna know! And that's what I wanted to *say*. But I was too scared of their answer. That night I went to bed in a room I shared with the three older boys. There were two sets of bunk beds and I had one of the top bunks. I didn't get much sleep as my head pounded and my brain raced and my pillow grew sopping wet with tears.

I'm not sure how long I stayed in this home, maybe a couple weeks, but it seemed like forever, and every night I would plan my getaway – even though I knew it was impossible. But occupying myself this way helped to offset and distract from my underlying fear that I'd never see my family again.

Then one day my foster parents told me I would be going home. In my young life I'd never felt such relief – in getting back to the life I knew and, for better or worse, the life to which I'd grown accustomed. That very day I was picked up and brought back to the same office with the harsh lights and steel furniture. I sat in a chair in the hallway near a window. I had one eye on the traffic outside and another eye on that same lady who had driven me to the foster home. She was busy shuffling papers at her desk. She seemed nervous. And I realized why when I saw my father's car pull into the parking lot. But I wasn't nervous or angry or sad or any of that. I was just happy to see someone I recognized. Now I felt like everything would be okay.

The lady was probably shocked that my father wasn't in prison.

He greeted me with a lopsided grin and a casual hug. Not that I'd expected anything more. And I didn't exactly leap into his arms either. We got in his car and started off – but not in the direction of our house. We were driving through a neighborhood I didn't recognize, which made me tentative, since I'd had enough of new neighborhoods for a while.

My father was taking me to his second house.

Where lived his second family.

I know what you're thinking – another wife and kid. Wrong. You say a wife and two kids on the side? Wrong again. Try another wife and *three* young children. To match the other three he'd had with the woman he'd just put in the hospital. Though several years younger than the originals, they consisted of two boys and a girl like me and my siblings, with olive skin and dark eyes, and the eldest boy of this parallel family had my first name! Now, I'm not sure what professionals would say are the psychological ramifications of this type of situation, but my basic feeling was that I had been singled out for replacement! (The other two kids didn't bear the names Margie or Billy – both of whom would join me later at the new house.) The entire introduction was a punch in the gut followed by a cold hard slap to the face. I was too scared to challenge my father because it would have only led to a beating, but I was filled with hatred and resentment of him and these . . . imposters.

From the outset I could tell that we were unwelcome. Based on conversations I overheard while there, it was clear that his new wife – I thought of her that way, but as it turned out bigamy was one sin my father had yet to commit – was not happy having additional kids in her house. A house much nicer than ours. Everything clean and shiny. The furniture still had that new smell to it and the kitchen was stocked with good food, even with cookies and other treats my mother couldn't afford. The children had lots of toys and nice clothes. So too the woman but she was always bitching and moaning about whatever thing it was she *didn't* have, while tending to every minuscule need of her little darlings. A chronic whiner. I didn't like her owing to the circumstances, but I wouldn't have liked her anyway.

As the days went on, I could tell that our being there put a strain on their relationship. It wasn't long before we were back home with our mother, who had been released from the hospital and appeared to be getting her strength back. But we had to promise our father, under threat of violence, not to divulge anything about his other family. It was *our* secret.

Only decades later did I learn what transpired during this period. Based on the police report one might imagine that my father would have been indicted and likely found guilty of attempted murder. But when my mother finally regained consciousness some days after the beating, she immediately asked about her kids and was told that my father had been arrested and we were all in foster homes. Separate ones. Of course we'd been sent to the foster homes not only because my father was in jail but because they were doubtful my mother would ever pull through. She was on the brink of death. And my mother feared that if she died then we kids would be forever separated. So she refused to press charges against my father and he was never hauled up before a court.

Though my mother did recover from the beating, the other bad news was that she had been given a tainted blood transfusion and contracted hepatitis B while in the hospital. The Health Department placed a red QUARANTINE sign on our front door warning of a health risk inside. Feeling ashamed we promptly tore it down each time, only to see it appear again the next day. Of course neither I nor my siblings understood the added health risks associated with a severely compromised immune system – not to mention the negative impact it had on her state of mind. We were just happy to be reunited and home. Things seemed normal again.

It was within a day of returning home that our maternal grandparents arrived in town. My mother was still weak and frail and needed help around the house. Our grandparents also did their best to distract us so that my mother could get her needed rest. I recall going to the Thrifty drugstore a few nights a week for nickel ice-cream cones. This was a special treat we enjoyed as long as my grandparents stayed. It was summer and they took us to the zoo and amusement parks. Sometimes our mother was strong enough to join us. Then after a couple weeks our grandparents left. This caused us to focus once more on our mother and we realized she was not the same. She seemed defeated. Periodically she would show the same energy, wit and feistiness that we were used to, but those instances were few and far between. The hepatitis caused her eyes to have a creepy yellow tint and she needed rest often.

It was teeming with kids on Penfield Avenue, so we spent lots of time outside playing. With the exception of my family it was a quiet neighborhood with small houses and mostly friendly neighbors. We rode our bikes and played football and baseball in the street. At one end of the block was a big field that the kids had turned into a dirt-bike course with little jumps and other "motocross" features. Flanking one side of the field was a high cement wall the other side of which was a large compound called The Crippled Children's Society – a home to kids with various afflictions. We had a couple friends whose parents lived and worked at the place, so we'd sometimes scale the wall and knock on their door. Their names were Henry and Raymond Sainz, but we called them "Froggy" and "Moon Dog." They were older than us by a couple years, funny guys, and they teased each other relentlessly.

The compound was sometimes a tough place to visit.

Seeing some of those kids with horrific physical and mental illness could be difficult. Periodically the compound had parties when all the kids were gathered in one place. I went to one of those parties with my brother, basically to hang out with Froggy and Moon Dog, and it was hard for me to watch the handicapped kids interact. Henry and Raymond were used to it so they were their normal selves. But seeing these kids had a profound effect on me. Any time I thought how bad my family life was, or felt sorry for myself, I would think of those kids at the party, many in wheelchairs and with severe mental disabilities, and suddenly my life wasn't so bad. I had the use of both my arms and legs, could speak normally, ride my bike and play sports. I was far more fortunate than those poor kids. I also knew that once I grew up I could escape my hell. These kids had a life sentence. I still see their faces today.

Four

TOUGH GUY

My father had a single aspiration for me – to be tough. Cold, callous and street-wise were preferable traits. He expected me to become an outfit guy and that was all there was to it. School? A waste of time. Sports? For sissies. He taught me that it was okay to lie or be lied to, steal or be stolen from and cheat or be cheated – that these were not moral issues but matters of savvy and street smarts. You trusted no one! At the same time he was something of a biblical scholar. He was always citing The Good Book – albeit with little interpolations of his own. Among his favorites were "Do unto others before they get a chance to" and "The meek shall inherit the earth – six feet of it!"

It was common for him to pull up in his Cadillac while I was playing with the neighborhood kids and shout from the car: "Who's the toughest kid on the block?" I knew what he wanted me to say, so I'd say it – "I am" – while staring hard at the other kids. My father would just sit in the car hoping for someone to disagree. Some did, most did not – partly because they were afraid of my father and partly because they were afraid of me. I *was* tough, having endured so many beatings from my father. There was nothing any kid could do to me that my father hadn't done tenfold. Sometimes

I received multiple beatings for a single offense. You see, my father had this bizarre habit of pacing up and down the hallway just outside of our bedrooms, muttering profanities to himself about what we had done to upset him, all the while becoming increasingly loud and angry until he barged in and administered more corporal punishment. It was fairly terrifying listening to this play out and anticipating when he might reenter the room. The good news is that we were never "grounded," if you want to see a bright side to this behavior, and of course I was desperate to.

He took great pleasure in playing the toughest-kid-on-the-block game every time we moved into a new neighborhood. It became a rite of passage and I hated him for it. Which meant I was growing both tough and *mean*. By the age of ten I could not only take a punch but deliver one even harder and promised myself that some day when I got big and strong enough I would give him a taste of his own medicine. Once I worked myself into that mindset, I could smash any kid in my way. Don't get me wrong, I didn't go looking for trouble, but I just never avoided it. My father couldn't have been more pleased, unaware of the hate and resentment I was building up for him inside.

Although I was certainly the toughest for my age and weight, one time there was this kid who was new to the neighborhood. He was bigger and had two or three years on me. My father pulled up and he saw the kid – a fresh challenge: "Who's the toughest kid on the block!" He puffed on his cigarette, blowing the smoke out the window and waiting to see what would happen. This time I didn't say anything. I learned later that my father had met the kid's father and so he knew the kid's name. "Hey Tim," he yelled. "Can you take down Johnny?" Then he gave me that look which said you either beat his ass or I'll beat yours. So I lunged toward Tim.

How could I have known that he had a pair of scissors behind his back? Maybe Tim's dad had sensed something when he met my father. In any case Tim came ready. He lifted his hands to ward off my attack and the scissors punctured my wrist. It was deep. Blood was squirting all over the place. This even scared my father. He scrambled out of the car, scooped me up and raced me to the Emergency Room.

I thought I was going to get a beating for not taking Tim down, but the blood and the stitches made my dad forget about the whole thing, and it wasn't long afterward that he stopped playing the who's-the-toughest-kid-on-the-block game. Besides – mission accomplished. I had become mean, tough and fearless. A badass just like he wanted.

Although I fought a lot with the kids on my block, we always seemed to quickly get over any grudges and go back to playing together. My best friend at the time was a guy named John Visciglia who went to the same school and lived a few streets down. He was a big Italian kid with an equally big heart which he wore on his sleeve. He had two older brothers, Pat and RJ, who were consummate ballbreakers. His parents were divorced and I remember his father was a prop master at one of the Hollywood studios. John encouraged me to join Little League Baseball as well as Pop Warner Football and Basketball. My mother signed me up, and John and I were on the same football team (Woodland Hills Cowboys) and the same basketball team. During the season all we ever did was talk about our last game or upcoming games. Competing in organized sports kept me busy and out of trouble. Although weakened by her recent ordeal, my mother always managed to get me to and from practices and games. Or she'd arrange transportation with the parent of a teammate. I don't recall my mother ever missing a game or my father ever attending one.

I remember my first day at Parkman Junior High. We'd just made one of our frequent moves and now I had to start making friends all over again. That first day my mother drove us to school where we met with administrators who showed us around. When we got to the cafeteria they explained where we needed to pick up our tickets for a free hot lunch. Standing in line I found myself with mostly black kids bused in from the black neighborhoods – and it wasn't long before I was mixing it up with them. We were playing basketball at recess and as a ball headed out of bounds the kid attempted to deflect the ball off me so it would only then go out of bounds and his team still retain possession. In such a situation, basketball's unwritten rule is you try to throw the ball off an opponent's leg.

Instead this kid fired it off my face while calling me a "honky bitch." I responded with every racial slur in the book – in both English *and* Italian. He charged me with his hands up and his fingers bent as if he had claws and started scratching me like a cat. He got through my guard but then I connected with a straight right to his chin. He dropped his head and I grabbed him in a headlock and swung him to the ground while continuing my verbal assault. One of the teachers broke us up but took notice of my foul language and hauled me to the principal's office.

The school couldn't reach my mother but somehow got in touch with my father. I'm guessing they had his number in my file from when I returned from my first foster home. The principal lectured me about fighting and the language I was caught using, but when he said my father was on his way over I was worried more about the principal than myself. Never yet had I gotten in trouble with him for fighting since he of course encouraged it, and when he arrived and the principal told him that I had beaten up a black boy while dropping multiple "N" bombs, my father spat: "So where's the colored kid?" The principal told him that he was back in class. My father looked at the scratches on my face and asked me if I had won and I nodded my head. He then accosted the principal and said in his hard Chicago accent that if the principal ever called him again about his kid winning a fair fight then he would put his *fucking* head through that *fucking* wall – lending added emphasis to this already emphatic statement by first jabbing his finger in the principal's face and then at the wall where said cranial insertion would take place. The principal was petrified and unable to speak. For a moment I thought he might have swallowed his tongue. He just stood there with his eyes bugged out and finally stuttered something unintelligible. Even though I thought it was funny, I contained my laughter since I thought it might be my turn next for having disrupted my father's day.

The next day I attended school as if nothing had happened.

During this same period my mom was often too sick to go to the store so she would ask me and my brother to go for her. One day she had us go buy some bread and milk. I expected her to hand me some cash but instead she gave me a booklet of food stamps. This is when I realized we were living on welfare. Adding to my shame, when I handed the checker in the store the stamps, I could sense the scorn of the adults behind us in line. The cashier herself gave us a condescending look. These and similar events caused me to notice how dilapidated things were in the house. The carpet, furniture, television and other items were old and beat up. Most of our clothes were worn and ratty, and the house was always a mess. I had already begun to compare the things we had with what I saw at my father's house, but now it was clear to me that we were outright poor!

And of course there was the other concern – my mother's drinking.

She no longer seemed interested in my sporting events and this saddened me. It also drove me to distraction, giving me migraine headaches that would last from one to two days and making it hard for me to concentrate at school and bring any real focus to my sporting activities. My father wasn't doing anything to help and my siblings seemed oblivious to the gravity of the situation. I felt it was all on my shoulders. Once at a 7-Eleven I ran across some fliers from Alcoholics Anonymous and then came home and strategically placed them around the house where she would be sure to find them. But she just threw them away and never said anything. Then one day it got to be too much. We were sitting in her old Rambler station wagon in the parking lot of the Gemco department store at Ventura and DeSoto, my brother and sister were in the store to buy something, and it was then that I pleaded with my mother to stop drinking. She turned to face me and put her hand on my arm saying in a soft voice that I was her favorite child. I was taken aback not only by what she said but how she said it. I told her that my teacher at school said parents love their children all the same. She just smiled at me and shortly thereafter my siblings returned to the car. To this day I am uncertain if she was sincere or just said this to change the subject.

There was a ray of hope when she began dating an older fellow named Jack Welch, a doctor in Encino. He was a nice man and truly cared about my mother. He recognized she had problems and tried to help. My mother was stubborn, however, and would not be told what to do. Things started to spiral downward rapidly. My mother periodically became so ill that she would end up in the hospital for a couple days. Likely guided there by Dr. Jack Welch. Whenever this happened a social worker would come to my class and take me to a foster home for a day or two.

As the weeks and months passed, she became weaker and lacked the will to control us kids. We all took advantage of the absence of parental supervision. My sister Margie, older by two years, was becoming rebellious while also running with the wrong crowd. She was definitely the wild one during that time. My brother Billy, younger by two years, seemed not to have a full understanding of how seriously the situation had degraded. I spent a lot of time with him and no matter how bad things were I always looked out for him.

I admit I was no angel, but I was never out of control and was able to excel in the classroom. Though I did hang out with some kids who partied it up with pot and alcohol. I had a good friend at the time named Russell Sheppard, and we would drink beer and play ping pong in his garage. A couple beers were all I could really handle. But on one occasion I messed up big time. Someone had brought a new drink over to Russ's place – Ripple! I didn't realize how much I was drinking that night. I do remember my friend's older brother letting me try his head phones and listening to Black Sabbath as the room began to spin. When I closed my eyes it made it much worse. I ran out of the room into the backyard to heave my guts out and ended up sleeping at Russ's house. The next day I woke up feeling queasy and with a monster headache. When I realized I had football practice that morning, I called my house and asked my mom to bring my equipment to Russ's house. She brought over my gear and dropped me off at practice. I threw up a couple times at practice but somehow got through it. The coaches just thought I was sick, not realizing their free-safety was a hungover 12-year-old. All it took was that one incident for me to start imposing strict self-control. And of course seeing what alcohol was doing to my mother. Her health was steadily deteriorating. Some days she would lie on the couch in the front room with a bucket by her side so she wouldn't have to run to the bathroom to vomit. Toward the end of the summer of '74 she began to vomit blood. We would take turns emptying the bucket. This is not how normal people lived, I thought. It was all very upsetting, and the only good part was that my father very seldom came around now.

Then one day he put in another spectacular appearance. My brother and I, along with some friends, were playing football in a field across the street from my buddy Russ's home. All of a sudden a car screeched to a halt and my father jumped out in a rage, screaming at me and my brother. He was carrying a short length of garden hose and proceeded to beat Billy with it. Our friends watched all this in horror and amazement. Horror because they had probably never seen anything so brutal in their lives; and amazement due to the sheer audacity of it – a man beating his own son in clear light of day for all to witness and with seeming unconcern. There was a passenger in the car who was taking it all in as well – my father's new woman and mother of his three new children. The look on her face told me that she was relishing the spectacle. Truly savoring it. The only thing she didn't do was run her tongue along her lips. It may sound strange but I blamed her more than my father. Why else would she be sitting there looking so gratified? Because she had revved him up!

Afterward I found out what had happened and it confirmed my hunch. My father had moved to a new house with his new family, and my brother Billy had written down the telephone number and then innocently forgotten it in his pants pocket. While doing the laundry my mother found the number and called it and had an ugly exchange with the homewrecker, who no doubt sicced my father on his own eleven-year-old son. From front to back it all pointed to her. I discovered only much later that this woman, Carol, had a long history with my father and had followed him from Chicago to California. According to my cousins she'd had a well-earned reputation in my neighborhood for being a slut of the first order. Even some of my father's family members openly referred to her as "that Lincoln Avenue whore."

One night in late August I brought my barbells into the front room to work out while watching TV. My mother was on the couch relaxing. She seemed exceptionally weak but engaged me in conversation. I told her I was working out for the upcoming football season. I was playing once again for the Woodland Hills Cowboys, having moved up from the Mighty Mite to the Jr. Midget division. I could tell she was struggling to talk and I immediately blamed her drinking. I started getting emotional and with my voice cracking told her she wasn't taking care of herself. She tried to change the subject, which triggered my frustration and I started crying and told her she was in fact killing herself. Again she weakly tried to change the subject. I finally reached my breaking point and uttered words that I will always regret: "I hate you!" I went back into my room crying. The next morning I rode my bike to Russ's place and spent most of the day at his house. I returned long enough to grab my pads and head to football practice at Taft High School, which was far but still walking-distance from my home.

I returned from football practice to an empty house. I wandered around the neighborhood looking for my brother and sister but was unable to find them. I made myself a bologna sandwich, watched TV and went to bed with an eerie feeling that something was very wrong. The next morning I was up early but still there was no one to be found. I watched TV to stop my mind from wandering, hoping someone in my family would soon show up. I heard a car pull into the driveway so I ran to the window hoping to see my mother.

Instead it was the woman from the office building with the steel furniture. At first I wasn't going to answer the door, pretending no one was home, but realized I was just delaying the inevitable. She was friendly and addressed me by name, though her upbeat demeanor made me uncomfortable because it gave me the feeling she was hiding something. I said very little as she told me to grab some extra clothes, that we were going back to the same family that had taken me in a few years earlier. She dropped me off and the overly friendly family greeted me in the front yard. Everything they said went in one ear and out the other. Emotionally I was defeated, so I made no effort to hide my sadness, but I did not cry. Perhaps I was past that stage because it felt more like anguish and despair. We entered the house where I continued to sulk for several hours. Then to my surprise, the very next day, they told me I was going home.

We drove back to the social worker's office where my father was waiting. He appeared happy to see me, which was a red flag since it was so out of character, though I also thought it might be for the benefit of the social worker. But then this extra-nice behavior continued even after we exited the building and got into the car. Now I was certain something was not good. I feared the worst but said nothing as we drove off. All I could think about was the last words I had spoken to my mother. Looking out the window there was nothing familiar. We were going up some winding hills with really big houses. I was puzzled, not realizing my father and his other family had moved. I remember pulling into the driveway of this huge house in bewilderment, then my mind snapping right back to worrying about the fate of my mother. My younger brother was already in the house. He was worried too.

At first we thought this was just temporary, hoping to be reunited with our mother in a few days, but days turned into weeks and I came to the realization I was never going home and my mother might be gone forever. My father never said a word and we were too scared to ask. We were afraid of the answer and afraid of a beating if he didn't like the question. One night I noticed that Carol was wearing clothes I recognized as my mother's. This not only made me furious, it seemed to confirm my greatest fear. My mother was dead.

She had died on 20 September 1974, just a few weeks after we moved into my father's big new house. According to the death certificate it was due to "Hepatic Failure with Pneumonia" as a consequence of "Laennec's Cirrhosis" – translation: chronic alcohol poisoning and liver failure entailing lack of prothrombin, which enables clotting of the blood; with no clotting, she suffered a massive hemorrhage, and the final straw was pneumonia. This was a horrible way to die.

Five

WELCOME TO HELL

It is my understanding, in most civilized societies, that informing a young boy of the death of his mother is a common courtesy. I also have to believe that attending the funeral of a dead parent is important psychologically to a kid – or an adult for that matter. I'm no expert but I imagine there must be some bad long-term effects on those not afforded a chance to properly grieve the loss of a loved one. Since I did not become a serial killer, I have to assume that the negative impact in my case has not been of inordinate magnitude. But I will admit that for many years I found it difficult to empathize with other kids who complained how "unfairly" their parents treated them.

The weeks turned into months and not a word was uttered regarding my mother. I remembered only too well the horrible last words I had spoken to her. Any time that Billy or Margie brought up our mother, I walked away saying: "I don't want to talk about it." This had more to do with my own guilt rather than being a cold-hearted bastard, which some people believed, but in our family that honor had already been commandeered by my father. At one point he'd told Margie that our mother had run off to Europe with a boyfriend. It sounded like something he would say, but the absurdity of that lie was monumental, even for him.

Did he think we wouldn't someday discover the truth? Was he that self-complacent? That distanced from reality?

Living with my father and his new family was anathema. He had moved to Encino, a well-to-do suburb at the southern end of L.A.'s San Fernando Valley. Sure it was a nice house, but it was like being in a prison with really nice jail cells. We were treated much differently than his younger kids who were very spoiled. One thing I can say for certain is that as long as I lived there I never saw him raise a hand to them outside of a mild spanking if they got out of line. Nothing like the savage beatings we received and continued to receive while living under his roof.

There would be no more baseball, football or other sports I enjoyed and we were far from all our old friends. I did not mind and fully accepted doing chores around the house, but I found it more than irksome having to babysit his three younger kids – Carol (aka "Baby Carol"), John and Gino. Unlike most kids my age I could not wait for summer to end and school to start again just so as to escape being a live-in babysitter.

And outside of being verbally abusive toward this new woman of his, my father never beat her that I could see, nor did I ever discern any signs of physical abuse on her face or arms or legs. Periodically he may have roughed her up, but no full-fledged battery that would have left visible marks. Carol was an attractive woman – curvaceous, handsome features, and giving off a strongly seductive vibe. As most temptresses do. She didn't just strut her stuff but was very flirtatious, I mean over the top, and acted provocatively when other men were around.

Hate is not a strong enough word to describe my feelings toward Carol. You would have to mix it with loathing and scorn and then multiply by a hundred. While most guys would have fantasized about banging her, I fantasized about killing her. She was conniving, good at firing up my volatile father regarding anything her twisted mind might deem bad behavior on our part. He would become highly agitated listening to her complain, then take it out on us in spades.

I was starting the eighth grade at my eighth school, Portola Junior High in Tarzana, a part of town which was adjacent Encino and named after the selfsame ape-man invented by author Edgar Rice Burroughs, who had once owned a ranch on the land. Portola was very different from Parkman Junior High, where I'd had the fight with the black kid, and was a predominantly Jewish school – so much so that on Jewish holidays I was one of the few who showed up to class. The girl who played Cindy in the TV show *The Brady Bunch* would put in an appearance on these days as well. I remember taking the bus from the hills of Encino to the Portola school grounds. At the bus stop I would always meet Schotzi and Joji Barris. Their father was a designer and builder of classic cars you saw on TV. Two of his best known works were the Batmobile and that modified hearse from *The Munsters* television series. Schotzi was always flamboyantly dressed. He was a nice guy but seemed odd to a street kid like me. The first time I went to that bus stop, my first day at Portola, I boarded the wrong bus and ended up at Birmingham High School. I called my father from the nearest phone booth knowing how pissed off he would be, but when he picked me up he didn't seem too aggravated.

As we made our way back to Portola in my father's new Jaguar, he reached over with his right hand to change the radio station and brought his left hand with its cigarette away from the open window and onto the steering wheel but dropped the cigarette. In retrieving it he accidentally cut off a guy driving a semi-tractor. The guy was furious and pulled up on our right yelling profanities and motioning for us to pull over.

"I'm going to kill this no good cocksucker!" This declaration of my father's was accompanied by a suitably murderous look. He pulled in front of the truck and hit the brakes. I could smell the rubber as the truck driver slammed the brakes on his giant wheels. Never in my life did I see my father move so fast. The truck driver was exiting his elevated cab when my father kicked the door, smashing the cab window against the guy's head and the bottom of the door against his shin. He kicked it a second time and then pulled the injured driver to the ground and planted his stylish Italian boot square in the man's face. He left him in a bloody heap and motioned me back in the car. A couple bystanders went over to tend to the injured driver. I heard someone yell to call the cops. My father continued on with me to school and no cops ever materialized.

Over the two years that I attended Portola I did manage to make a few friends, but not a great many. I didn't feel like I fit in there, so I didn't make much of an effort. I maintained good grades but was still getting in fights, and for the first time in my life was given a detention for being disruptive in the classroom. When given a detention you were required to have a parent sign a slip indicating they were aware you would be staying after school. In an act of defiance I had my older sister forge the slip with the name of our dead mother. This didn't elude the school's attention and I was summoned by a counselor who reprimanded me and called our house but was essentially ignored. Since my father paid little mind to what I did in school, I never feared any recourse, especially where fighting was concerned.

In fact he would often have me ditch school to help with

his roofing jobs, which he was still doing for quick money between scams. Not that he worked up much of a sweat. He'd exaggerate how much work was needed, pick up a hammer, make a few taps here and there, throw some tar sealant around the chimney, inflate the cost of supplies and labor, then collect from the clueless homeowner. The sweating was *my* job. I'd haul bundles of shingles up the ladder, pass my father whatever tool he needed, and handle the cleanup duty. My "pay" was a candy bar or a comic book, usually not both.

It was after one certain job that my father went to collect his money and the suspicious female homeowner started giving him grief. She questioned the quality of his work and the price of the materials. When my father pushed back, she demanded to see his contractor's license, which of course he didn't have. My father got madder and madder, but I could tell he wasn't nervous about being busted for no license; he wasn't afraid of the authorities, he was afraid of not getting paid.

So he told her his license was in the truck, that he'd go and get it. As we walked to the truck he told me to climb back on the roof and pretend to follow up on the homeowner's request to check the quality of the work. He told me to walk to the edge of the roof and fall off. Come again? I looked at him like he was crazy. "Just do it!" came his tight-lipped reply. I didn't argue. Cursing him, I climbed on the roof searching for a spot reasonably close to the ground and where I could land on grass. I looked down and saw my father becoming increasingly pissed with the lady – and presumably with me for taking so long. I worked my way to the edge, picked out my landing area, then pretended to slip. But I needn't have pretended because I had overlooked the rain gutter. My foot caught on the thing and changed the angle of my fall and instead of landing on relatively soft grass I slammed down on a strip of concrete with my knee striking a sprinkler head.

The only upside is I didn't have to feign an injury.

I was in agony.

From start to finish it was very realistic.

I grabbed my knee and couldn't see the lady's reaction since my eyes were shut tight in pain. But I sure could hear her. She was freaked out: "Is he okay? Is he okay?" As my father carried me to the truck, he said, "I don't know, but it looks bad. I think he broke his leg. I gotta take him to the hospital. I'll let you know." He also made sure to inform her that I was underage, a scare tactic, since it would probably cause a problem with a minor being injured on her property. I never went to the hospital, my leg wasn't broken, but I did have a nasty bruise in the shape of a sprinkler head on my knee.

That night the lady called our house, concerned about my condition but mostly about a potential lawsuit. My father told her that I was in a cast, my leg busted up, and it worked like a charm.

Under my father's tutelage I had pulled off my first successful caper. To him this was a far greater accomplishment than anything I had ever done in school. My biggest concern was that if the lady wanted proof of my injury, my father might enter my room at night and crack me in the knee with a hammer! But it never came to that and the woman ended up paying extra.

It was on the eve of America's bicentennial that my paternal grandfather's health began to fade. Before he died he wanted to travel to California to see his son one last time. Travelling with him were some aunts and uncles and a couple of my cousins, Jerry and Mike. Shortly after their arrival my grandfather's condition took a turn for the worse. When I saw him he looked very ill and did little but rest. My cousins and

I watched him in shifts because, among other illnesses, he had cirrhosis and was constantly vomiting. Mike and I would take turns emptying his bucket – just as I had done two years earlier for my mother. Though my grandfather's cirrhosis wasn't alcohol-induced, it still caused me to remember the last words I had spoken to her and revisit my sorrow on that count.

My grandfather passed away in February of 1976, just a few weeks after he had arrived in California. Surprisingly my father paid for us to fly to Chicago and attend the wake and funeral. The wake was a two-day affair and there had to have been several hundred people going in and out of the funeral home. I saw many of the aunts, uncles and cousins whom I had neither seen nor heard from in years. For the next few days I stayed with my cousin Mike in his basement room at my aunt Arlene's North Chicago two-flat – the same basement room which would become my summer home for the next four years.

The day before the funeral Mike drove me to All Saints Cemetery where the Costellos had a sizeable family plot. Over it hovered a large statue of Jesus with a polished block on each side, one engraved with "Costello" and the other with the real family name of "Gagliardi." One of the first graves I noticed was my uncle Paul who had been shot to death a couple years earlier. This led to a discussion between me and Mike about what we thought actually happened the day he was killed.[2] Then we returned to the car and Mike said he was

---

2 On 13 August 1974 my uncle Paul Andrzejczak was shot to death in the hallway of his North Chicago home while his three children slept. Paul was the husband of my father's sister Linda – aka the "Merry Widow." There was tremendous controversy surrounding the shooting, and while it was eventually ruled self-defense, questions remained. Many of my family believed that Linda had set up our unsuspecting uncle – since the killer was also her lover. A guy named Karanickis. We were convinced that the witnesses lied; their stories just didn't add up. But Paul was considered a "bad apple" and was the known associate of a double cop-killer. Needless

going to make one more stop before heading for home. He drove several miles to another cemetery called Saint Joseph's and we got out and he led me to a grave and pointed to the headstone.

I tried to hold my emotions in check but could not. I walked a few feet away and turned my back to hide the tears. It was one thing to know your mother was dead, it was an entirely different matter to see the tombstone with her name on it. Perhaps the fact that no one sat me down to say *Sorry kid, bad news, your mother died today*, and this combined with not being given the chance to say a final goodbye, only served to intensify the moment.

The upshot was I returned to California with a larger chip on my shoulder than when I had left. I found it more difficult than ever to accept living with my father and his new brood. There was an overwhelming feeling of guilt that I had somehow betrayed my mother and her side of the family by accepting her/our fate without a fight. So I started making up for it by being more mouthy and combative with both my father and Carol. As far as I was concerned she was just as guilty as him. Adding insult to injury, there were many times when other kids and adults unknowingly referred to Carol as my mother. I would immediately notify them in a disdainful way that she wasn't anything close. The merest reference to my "stepmother" made me crazy! Anything with the word mom or mother in it was a constant reminder that mine was dead. And hearing the name of their eldest son – "John" – always gave rise to that feeling of having been replaced. Though hardly in every sense. While I had been my father's experimental lab rat – or more aptly a trained fighting

to say, the Chicago police and DA had little motivation in pursuing the case. But Karinickis got his comeuppance, later squashed by a truck. Since my father threatened to stick a knife in Karinickis's eye during a telephone conversation weeks before, rumors swirled around my father's possible involvement in his demise.

dog from whom he could periodically derive some sick entertainment value – he *never* pulled that who's-the-toughest-kid-on-the-block shit with the new John or with Gino. Not in this upper-class neighborhood. I'm sure Carol had something to do with that not only because these were her little treasures but she didn't want to alienate her affluent neighbors.

She hadn't minded at all seeing my brother getting flayed.

One evening at dinner she started in with me on some petty bullshit – this time for leaving dirty dishes in the sink.

"What's it matter to you," I said. "You've got a live-in maid."

"She has other things to do."

"Like what – fluff up your satin pillows and dust off your diamonds?"

I had never hidden my flat-out hatred for Carol – a hatred which my father tolerated to a certain extent. He knew there was no way of tamping that down. As long as I wasn't blatantly disrespectful. And injecting some humor also helped. This time I even thought to see the barest hint of a smile on his lips – Carol's tastes were expensive and they were tastes for which he had to foot the bill.

"How dare you!" she said.

"Go fuck yourself."

This could be termed blatantly disrespectful.

Any semblance of amusement on my father's face immediately vanished and he reached over and grabbed me by the back of the neck. And for the first time in my life I resisted. I flung off his arm. That was a mistake. But only because I didn't follow up by punching him in the face. I wasn't mentally ready for that. He pulled me from my chair and threw me to the ground and kneeled over me cursing and hitting me hard with an open hand. Since I had taken worse beatings in the past from his knuckles this was mild by comparison. But I learned my lesson. Before shooting off my mouth I had to be ready to commit to a full-on fight.

Another thing came of that incident – it made clear to me that I wanted to spend next summer back on the north side of Chicago with my cousins and away from the hell I was currently living. There was resistance at first – after all, I was part of the live-in help. But my father could see my increasingly brazen disdain for Carol and his new family, and in addition I was getting older, bigger and more difficult to control. He was also keenly aware that I had a temper on par with his own. I could snap one day and do something drastic. The dinner incident might be just a small harbinger of things to come.

This is the chief reason, I believe, why he allowed me and my younger brother to spend that first summer and subsequent ones in Chicago.

Little did I know the insanity awaiting me in that city.

Six

While my paternal grandfather was alive he had his hands full keeping my crazy grandmother in line, as she was constantly trying to run her kids' lives. She was also violent and thought nothing of throwing a brick through a rival's window or cracking someone over the head with a high-heeled shoe. A rabble-rouser of the first order, she liked to pit her kids and in-laws and cousins against each other – and you took her side or risked being placed on that week's enemy list. If someone outside the family made that list then she was even quicker to avenge the perceived injury. (Her attitude - nobody was going to screw with a Costello and get away with it!) either personally or through a phone call to someone else in the family who would then take prompt action.

We called her "Ma" to her face and "CL" behind her back - short for Crazy Lady.

It was not long after my grandfather's death that all hell broke loose. And I witnessed the chaos first-hand since I remained in Chicago the entire summer after my grandfather's funeral and every summer thereafter until my freshman year of college. And when I say first-hand I mean first-hand, since I lived in my grandmother's basement that initial summer. Within days of my arrival, she learned that some older kid was bullying one of my younger cousins. She drove us to the park where my cousin identified the kid and I gave him a beating. Then we got back in the car and drove home and she made us a nice meal. Oh boy, I thought, room and board as her live-in enforcer.

The notion had been to spend the summer in Chicago so as to escape my father and his madness, but I'd forgotten that he must have inherited his crazy-gene from someone and that someone wasn't my grandfather. (He was carrier of the crime-gene.) My father and my grandmother both possessed the same twisted logic, and even the mannerisms and body language were similar. When she became angry she would curse and wave her hands wildly. During a scathing conversation about someone, she would signal her agreement by poking me in the side with her elbow and say "ain't it, ain't it" (short for ain't it the truth) about every two minutes until I thought she'd cave in a rib. A habit picked up by several of my relatives. Some repeated this mannerism involuntarily whereas others, like the cousins my age, did it in mockery.

I could go on and on about my grandmother, but suffice it to say that when she died at ninety or thereabouts, my cousin Mike and I waited an extra half hour at the cemetery not to mourn privately but to make certain that she was really and truly dead. We believed this she-devil was immortal, and as we stared at the newly dug grave we were certain a hand would emerge from the loose dirt and she would pull herself up and make her way to the reception and whip up a family fight about the funeral arrangements they'd made for her.

Being cooped up with this insanity, and since I missed competitive sports, I took every opportunity to leave the house and started visiting a CYO (Catholic Youth Organization) gym where I first learned boxing fundamentals. Before then I'd just been a tooth-and-nail streetfighter. But now I figured it would be smart to polish my skills in light of what I knew might be facing me back in the neighborhood – or what I might be pushed into by my grandmother. To earn money I worked as a roofer with my cousins and uncles on my father's side. Three of them had roofing businesses and I worked with all three crews one time or another but mostly with my cousin Mike and his stepfather Paul. The work was backbreaking, and you've never experienced heat and humidity until you've roofed houses during a remorseless Chicago summer. During the week we would work all day and then at night either cruise the neighborhood, hang out at the park, or drive to the lake and throw down beers. The lake was where the underaged went to drink and where you could find any drug from A to Z. There was always gang activity, fights and street races, and as self-styled tough guys me and my cousins waded into more than a few altercations.

Because of the drug-dealing and street-racing, the cops would break things up and send people home at 11 pm. They were basically imposing a curfew. Any defiance resulted in a good ass-kicking or a ride in the paddy wagon and a booking for disorderly conduct. Unless of course the cops were in a bad mood. In that case you would be dropped off in a less than desirable neighborhood where you had to make it back in one piece. No easy task. Remember this was before cell phones, and in those days Chicago was extremely segregated. Nobody liked outsiders in their part of town, gangs were on the prowl, and you were usually identified by your ethnicity. But the 11 pm curfew worked well for me and Mike during the week because we had to be up early the next morning anyway for a long day of demanding labor.

Saturday mornings we could sleep an extra hour or two but then Mike and I had to mow the grass at his house and that of his elderly neighbor. When done there we drove a few blocks to my crazy grandmother's house (I'd only lived there the first few weeks) and mow her lawn as well, and afterward we might buy some rubber balls at the Rexall and play "fast pitch" in the schoolyard. Fast pitch was similar to "wall ball" but you use a full size bat. You could play two-on-two with a pitcher and outfielder. A strike zone was spray-painted or chalked on the side of a brick building so the wall acted like a catcher and bounced the ball back to the pitcher after each pitch. The rules were just like line ball. On Sundays I mowed the lawn of my maternal grandparents. Grandpa Mac always had odd jobs for me to do around their house. Usually cleaning and painting rain gutters, window frames and his back porch. "If there's one thing I hate, it's a lazy bastard," he'd say while handing out my chores for the day and then kicking back with a stiff drink to watch the televised Cubs game.

After my chores were through I liked sitting around and just talking to the guy. He'd usually still be in his favorite armchair watching TV and I'd join him, making certain to put something over my spot on the sofa so as not to get it dirty. During the commercial breaks were teasers for the news that followed the game. Sometimes these teasers spoke of police corruption, which prompted my (by now) more-than-slightly-inebriated Grandpa Mac to add colorful insight. He told stories of infamous Chicago events like the killing of John Dillinger at the Biograph Theater, the Saint Valentine's Day Massacre, and other crime stories. However the most vivid association I have with Grandpa Mac, apart from his not-so-subtle contempt for my father, was a conversation we had where he told me that when he became a cop one of his first busts was for a robbery. He caught the perp fleeing the scene and tackled him; the perp offered him money to let him go but my grandfather refused it; so the perp promptly paid off the sergeant and walked. Grandpa Mac revealed that almost everyone was on the take – it simply got more expensive as things moved up the law-enforcement food chain – up to and including judges. What I found most fascinating was the prevailing attitude of his instructors at the police academy, one of whom told my grandfather that because it was difficult to get by on your paycheck, on the street "you take what you're worth." In my book Grandpa Mac was priceless. One afternoon as we sat and watched TV, an Alcoholics Anonymous commercial came on. At the end of the commercial a concerned voice said: "If you don't call us, you have to call someone." Grandpa Mac was already half in the bag at this point, and with drink in hand he looked at me and said, "You know those fucking alcoholics give us drunks a bad name!"

Sometimes our work during the week would be rained out. On those days I visited other relatives. For instance my cousin Jimmy in a different Chicago neighborhood than my own. Jimmy was the first son of my father's sister Adele and around my age. Once while I was sitting on his porch, waiting for him to return home, I was confronted by some locals who were older than me asking what I was doing on their street. They tried to intimidate me. But when they realized I wasn't associated with any gang but still willing to fight, they changed their tune. The biggest kid handed me a business card that read *White Knights*. It had the kid's name on it and at the top read: *We fight for the right to keep it all white.* He said the Blackstone Rangers were making their presence felt in the area and that something was needed to counter this black gang. I got the impression they wanted to recruit me so I feigned interest but told them I was from a neighborhood too far away. Not that I would have joined anyway, since I had never been taught to hate minorities. Not even from my father, who was hardly pure as driven snow. His reasoning had always been that an asshole was an asshole or a sucker a sucker no matter their race. An equal-opportunity hustler. But in those days the gangs tended to be organized along ethnic lines, each wanting people outside of their group to be kept outside of their neighborhoods. So there was always ethnic bashing and banter but it was the way everyone spoke. I was called a greasy dago, guinea wop and other such things but it never bothered me. You laughed it off as did those of other ethnic backgrounds – Micks, Polacks, Spics – because we were just street kids far removed from the world of bullshit politics. Using an ethnic slur, whether in jest or in anger, had little meaning for us personally but was a rough way of expressing your affection for a person or baiting them into a fight. You just wanted to trigger a reaction, you didn't hate an entire ethnic group. That would take a lot of energy. I had enough to do just hating my immediate family.

I'll admit that when dealing with black guys it was a touchier subject. But even then, if you were friends, you could throw all kinds of stuff each other's way. And I did have black friends along with friends from other assorted minorities, both then and later.

I have no idea what happened to the White Knights after my encounter with them, but there were still many gangs in Chicago at the time. You had the Almighty Popes, Royals, Latin Kings, C-Notes, Howard Street Greasers and others who had "sweaters" and carried business cards with their names and logos and slogans. My introduction to corporate America. The Blackstone Rangers were considered a black "separatist" group and morphed into a Muslim organization called El Rukyn. You could usually tell whose turf you were on by the graffiti on the walls and garage doors and such. We knew many gangbangers but mostly hung out with the Popes, as a couple of my cousins and several friends were members, though most of my friends and cousins remained unaffiliated.

If we were not at the lake then we cruised the neighborhood streets, during which I realized that Chicago was far different from Los Angeles. First and foremost the people are of a harder sort and not terribly cordial, possibly due to the long harsh winters, but they were equally unfriendly in the spring, summer and fall. In most neighborhoods a blue-collar atmosphere reigned, the people I hung out with always seeming to be on edge. And the things we got away with were unthinkable in California. There was the one time I was cruising around the North Side with my cousins and we got pulled over by the local police. We all had beers in our laps. As I attempted to hide mine, I noticed the others made no effort. We were all underage and driving with open containers – a real no-no in So Cal! The cop came to the driver's side, looked in the back seat and rolled his eyes: "Can't you guys drink somewhere we can't find you?" Then he told us to go drink at the park. Didn't even make us pour our beer out.

It was pretty obvious that unless you committed a serious crime, you were given a pass. One time we were sitting in the park around 10 pm drinking beer when a spotlight was flashed on our group. While being directed to a designated area it became clear that the person on the police speaker was a woman. Then she exited the car and it was not only a woman but a diminutive one. She told us to turn around and face the closest car in our vicinity, which turned out to be my cousin Mike's newly painted Buick. She grabbed the purse of one of the girls we were with and then made the mistake of setting it on the hood of Mike's car. Mike objected and the female cop said, "Calm down tough guy!" Mike had a short fuse and began cursing the cop and flung the purse across the street. The female cop then attempted to handcuff Mike, which was comical, as Mike just stood there with his 220 pounds of hard muscle – we didn't call him Iron Mike for nothing – and refused to be cuffed. We all started laughing. She called for backup. We could have easily run away but didn't – this was too entertaining. As two additional squad cars arrived the female cop was immediately reprimanded by the ranking male officers who knew us from the neighborhood. As she drove off, the male officers shook their heads and after some casual conversation they left. Confirming my theory that they had far more important things to do than harass some neighborhood ruffians peacefully drinking beer in the park – the very place where we'd originally been directed by the Chicago police!

Sometimes on Monday nights we would go over to our cousin Ronnie's for football. Ronnie was the son of CL's sister Ginny, who was fairly crazy herself, but in a non-threatening and fun way. Ronnie was older but liked hanging out with his Costello cousins, especially me and Mike. His nickname was "mouse" because he was small and at one time had lived in our basement when we were infants. Ronnie was a complete stoner. The guy was never not high. He drank beer, too, in quart bottles. We had a standing prank we played on Ronnie. He was always so stoned by the time Mike and I arrived at his apartment that Mike would introduce me by a different name and as a friend of his rather than the blood relative Ronnie had long known. Ronnie would say hi and address me by the phony name. It took a few minutes of conversation for Ronnie to catch on to the gag. One day we arrived at Ronnie's to learn that his nephews had stolen the battery from his car, an early model Pontiac Firebird. From his window onto the alley he had watched them pop his hood and yank the battery out. These certain nephews were Munchie and Mike, real pond scum, the worst of the worst when it came to the white trash on my father's side. These two losers were heavy into heroin and lived in the projects. They made the mistake of calling Ronnie after the deed to warn him not to tell Iron Mike. The problem was that Iron Mike and I happened to be at Ronnie's at the time and Iron Mike answered the phone. He gently told them that we were on the way over to "knock the fuck" out of them. We drove to their shithole neighborhood which was essentially a Puerto Rican ghetto and busted through the door. It was one of the most disgusting places I've ever seen, filthy with rotting food on the table and trash everywhere. I saw at least two rats scurry across the floor as we barged in. Bed sheets were being used as curtains. There were rusty spoons and old hypodermic needles lying around. We looked at each other and shook our heads. Then we went checking the rooms in search of these dirt bags. In the disgusting bathroom there was a yellow-pages phonebook with about half the pages torn out because they were using it as toilet paper.

We didn't find them, but the next day Ronnie's battery had been returned, fully installed.

Several years later, Ronnie died of brain cancer at 38 years old. Munchie and Mike met a predictable fate. One overdosed on heroin, while the other died in a mental hospital of complications from extended drug use.

When cruising the streets of our Chicago neighborhood we were always on the lookout for hostile parties. Although most of my cousins weren't gang members, there were enough of us to discourage any gangs from causing trouble in our neighborhood. A mutual respect existed, so there weren't many confrontations. However one of the guys in the Costello family cross-hairs was a witness to the 1974 killing of my uncle Paul. He was a friend of the gunman Don Karanickis, who was killed roughly a year later in a freak motorcycle accident. Some believed it was a suicide, but at one point my father was questioned because I remember eavesdropping on a telephone call and hearing him say, "How the hell could I have killed him when I'm three thousand miles away!" I presumed a detective was at the other end of the line.

Anyway it was our strong belief that the witness had lied to police during the investigation so as to help his friend. Any time we thought to recognize his car – a black and yellow Pontiac 442 – a chase ensued. In one instance my cousin Mike and I were going to pick up some food and beer to bring back to Ronnie's place before watching a football game. Ronnie gave Mike the keys to his Pontiac Firebird, which Mike liked to drive. As we made our way to the store Mike recognized the 442 driving in the other direction and pulled a fast (illegal) U-turn, tires screeching, and the chase was on. Mike gunned the motor and we were closing in when a construction zone loomed. The tires on Ronnie's car were a bit worn and couldn't handle the speed in combination with the layer of gravel strewn across the road. The car fishtailed while Mike overcorrected and we wound up wrapped around a telephone pole. Neither of us was wearing seatbelts so we were thrown around with Mike getting the worst of it as he took the impact of the pole to his left while I crashed into the right door panel. We ran from the scene. When we got far enough away we ducked into a phone booth to inform Ronnie that he needed to report his car as stolen. Then we called a friend who picked us up and drove us home.

Another day at the office.

Even though the work was hard and the potential for disaster high, I cherished summers in Chicago. There was always something exciting going on and we were always in the mix. I felt invincible and took stupid and unnecessary risks – and the feeling of risk was magnified by the fact that I was coming from the safe confines of Encino. Each year when I returned to California and shared summer stories with my high-school friends they thought I was full of it.

We won't be returning to this, so I want to conclude: It would be five straight summers humping heavy bundles of shingles up ladders all day in the sweltering heat with my favorite cousin Mike, and at the end of that time I had a tough and disciplined work ethic, had gained tremendous street knowledge, and was able to hone my fighting skills both on and off the pavement. My confidence was at an all-time high – as too was my anger and resentment.

Seven

Since I went to middle school for grades seven through nine, I entered high school in the tenth grade. This time my father had a surprise in store. He enrolled me at Crespi Carmelite High School in Encino, where we were living at the time, a private all-boys Catholic school with a total student body of some 400 kids. It was a surprise not only because Crespi was known for its fine academic and sports program – two things my father pretended to disdain – but there was fairly steep tuition, at least in comparison to the public high schools where tuition was zero. I had the brief thought that maybe he was starting to value my educational development, that through my grades and sporting successes I had nudged him into believing that I could be more than just a common street thug and that maybe this wasn't all bad.

But even if enrollment at Crespi looked good on the surface of things, I wasn't entirely grateful. Most of the kids graduating Portola Junior High were going on to attend Birmingham High School in Van Nuys, and most of the kids from my previous middle school, Parkman Junior High, were moving on to Taft High School in Woodland Hills. This meant that I was once more entering a new place without a single friend or acquaintance. For the first couple weeks I sat away from the other kids. What was the use? I'd probably get shunted to a completely different high school after a year of this one. If not earlier. One of the Catholic priests always greeted me whenever we passed in the school hallway. Sensing a problem, one day he engaged me in conversation, just small talk, but it encouraged me to interact with the other kids, which I knew I'd have to eventually. And it wasn't only this priest but the whole Crespi environment which was conducive to friendly interaction. With very few exceptions almost everyone associated with the school was amiable and supportive. It was easy to make friends in this atmosphere. And as I got to know these boys I quickly realized how truly screwed up my own family was. I became friends with many kids of Italian and/or Irish extraction like myself, but their parents and relatives were unlike mine, their homes little islands of peace and tranquility. Of course you had no idea what happened in their homes when you left, but at least nothing nasty went down while you were there. Unlike at my house where you were greeted with screaming and recriminations the minute you walked through the door. And at a certain point I didn't even care what went on behind the closed doors of my friends' homes – all I knew is that they provided needed relief from my own whacked-out household.

On the flipside I felt awkward due to questions posed by my newfound friends and their families. I would be sitting at the dinner table of a normal nuclear family and hear, "So John, what does your father do for a living?" Or maybe, "John, tell us about your mother." What was I going to say? *Well ma'am, in a nutshell, my father is a con-man and gangster who beat my mother so severely that she spent weeks in the hospital where she was given a tainted blood transfusion that caused her to contract hepatitis B and become so depressed that she turned to drinking and eventually died of cirrhosis of the liver. Please pass the potatoes.* Not a conversation I wanted to have. So I would always say my father was self-employed and that my mother had died of some liver disease – all true as far as it went.

The teacher who made the biggest impression on me that first year was Father Leo Glueckert. He was a real character and is best described as the Henny Youngman of Catholic priests – *Take my vows – please!* Father Leo taught late-modern European history and his course kicked off with the French Revolution. So that we could gain a more in-depth understanding of it, Father Leo orchestrated what he called a "classroom simulation" or learning game. It was essentially role-playing, but history didn't have to repeat itself; you could make your own decisions – and dig your own grave. Half the class was peasantry, a quarter were wealthy bourgeoisie, and the last quarter was divided between nobility and clergy. We drew names from a tricorne hat to see which group we belonged to and I was not only a nobleman but Louis XVI! Sounds good but the objective of the game was to better your standing, somewhat difficult to do when you're already king. But at least I could go the historical Louis one better – paying off the national debt and saving my head. Over the next couple weeks I was able to sniff out those who were intent on double-crossing me (wealthy bourgeoisie and many nobles) and I used members of the landed clergy to offer them lifetime absolution for their sins if they would only fork over the requisite dough to pay off the national debt. The nobles went for it. After my finance minister collected all their play money, I promptly had the landed clergy excommunicate these duplicitous jerks. The wealthy bourgeoisie didn't pay up, but I let them ride since I'd be needing them against cutthroats like Robespierre.

So I weathered the Revolution. It was only years later that Father Leo told me he had "gerrymandered" three key positions – Robespierre, Neckar the finance minister, and Louis XVI. Father Leo said that I had projected a certain "authority" and "regalness." But to be honest I think those were just nice words – what I think he really sensed were my street-smarts and well-honed instinct for survival.

Anyway that was Crespi for you – the teachers took a personal interest. And this was not only a revolution in my life but it made you at least *feel* like a king.

Part of the Crespi curriculum included forty hours of what they called "Christian Service" in which you donated your time helping others. There were a number of options, like going bowling with kids stricken by cerebral palsy or helping out at an old-folks home, and I chose to tutor a freshman in math. Another requirement was traveling to downtown Los Angeles and working at a soup kitchen for the poor and homeless. These programs were supposed to keep us kids appreciative and humble, but I'm afraid they had minimal impact on me because I was already hardened from my own family experiences. The things being preached at Crespi were diametrically opposed to what I'd undergone, and at a certain point I simply couldn't process it all. But the Crespi element in my life now caused me to examine what it was I held to be true, and I came up with a belief system that can best be described as God meets Poker meets Darwin.

I'd always believed in God but at certain times I thought he had abandoned me – as evidenced by all the negative things that were happening in my life. Then I recalled those poker games in the basement of my grandfather's house in Chicago. Sometimes you got a good hand and sometimes a bad one. The luck of the draw, just like life. Those kids at the Crippled Children's Society had drawn one lousy hand! Comparatively speaking, my hand wasn't that bad. I just needed to play it better. That's when I realized God created free will and it was on you to make the best of it. Though how I did that was not always in conformance with Catholic doctrine. I had grown up in a Darwinian world where only the fittest survived, so there was no way I was going to "turn the other cheek" – though I *was* starting to reassess my father's aggressively cynical "Do unto others before they get a chance to."

In our well-to-do area of Encino there was an armed private security guard who patrolled the neighborhood. He was a heavy-set guy who regularly drove by in his patrol vehicle and flashed his searchlight through our front windows - something which my father found unnecessary unless we were out of town. The security guard was repeatedly warned not to continue this practice unless given prior notice that the house was unoccupied. But he continued to do so in an almost defiant fashion. One night my father had enough, and after again seeing the bright lights flash into our dining room he ordered me to grab his keys and we jumped in the car. We caught up to the security guard and chased him for miles. He finally pulled into the closest police station and ran into the busy lobby believing to be safe in the presence of uniformed officers. He was speaking to a couple deputies and pointed his finger in our direction as we entered. My father was seething as he reached into his pocket to light a cigarette and I could hear the familiar muttering of profanities, signaling a violent episode was imminent. Walking toward the threesome, my father took a drag of his smoke and when he got within striking distance he removed the cigarette from his lips and planted the lit end on the forehead of the security guard. The two cops grabbed and cuffed my father while he managed to launch a bonus loogie in the face of the security guard:

"You fat pig, you should thank me I put that fire out on your face! You could have burned to death!"

They held my father for a couple of hours. He was

charged with assault and battery and released after posting a small bond. A couple weeks later the security guard thought better of it. He dropped the charges and came to our house apologizing. He even bought my father a gift. Ready for this? A Colt 38 Super Auto pistol! Made sense because if he wasn't going to be flashing his spotlight through our windows anymore then my poor defenseless father needed some way to protect himself against burglars . . .

But at least I was insulated from my father's antics at Crespi. Or so I thought. It was my junior year the time he picked up my younger half-siblings at the Catholic elementary school across the way from Crespi. The school had just let out and my father was driving slowly down the street as one does when small kids are running wild after dismissal. At the same time, on the Crespi side of the street, was a Crespi teacher who was using mild profanity in reprimanding a couple students. My father stopped his car and stuck his arm out the window with his hand outspread, that typically Italian gesture, and hollered: "OHHHHHH! Watch your language around my kids you stupid jagoff!" Now I don't know what the teacher's immediate reaction was (I got all this later from one of the bystanders who said they couldn't hear what the teacher replied — so at least he hadn't raised his voice) but whatever he said didn't satisfy my father who exited the car and grabbed him by the shirt and gave him a couple shakes. Upon being informed that he was assaulting one of the Crespi teachers, my father threw him to the ground and charged into the administrative office a few dozen steps away. Afternoon classes had just begun and I happened to be in the classroom closest to the administrative office, but as my father burst into the office seeking the principal Father John, I could have been at the other end of the building and still made out every last one of the profanities he was spewing so as to enter his complaint about a teacher who'd been spewing profanities. He ended with a flourish: "And if you don't straighten this motherfucker out then the next time you talk to him you'll be reading him his last fucking rites!"

It took only a couple minutes before Father John found me and pulled me from the classroom and into his office.

"Your father was here," he said, clearly shaken and slipping some pill into his mouth, probably to calm himself.

"I heard," I said. "Along with every other kid in school."

"Is he always like this when he gets angry?"

"No," I said, looking Father John over for signs of physical injury. "He's usually a lot worse."

Father John expressed concern about what he had just experienced. I told him not to worry, I was used to my father's lunacy, that nothing would come of the incident. And nothing did come of the incident – with the exception of every kid, teacher, administrator and coach at school eventually getting word of just how bat-shit crazy my old man was. And this episode only confirmed to those few friends of mine who had already met my father that he was in fact a bona-fide gangster. No one could be that ballsy without some heavy artillery behind him. The rumor spread to others at Crespi and by the time I was a senior most kids believed that my father was somehow involved with the mob. I took a lot of teasing, in English class some joker might say: *Hey Costello, what comes at the end of a sentence – an appeal!* Or they'd form comedy duos, like in math class, one guy starting out: *If Johnny's father had ten apples and his neighbor took five of the apples, what would Johnny's father have left?* – his buddy chiming in: *A dead neighbor and all ten apples!*

It was like I was in some corny vaudeville sketch. "Who told you there is a cement mixer on my father's boat?" That was the self-chosen caption to my senior photo in the yearbook. Because by this time I realized that having mob connections engendered respect and kept people from asking uncomfortable questions I wasn't inclined to answer. It also lent you a glamorous aura – what I call the "Godfather factor." The first two *Godfather* movies had only recently appeared, Hollywood making the underworld seem like this highly romantic deal, so it gave people a nervous thrill to believe I was son of a mobster.

But little did my new friends know that I was gravitating toward them largely to escape all that "glamour" they ascribed to me. They all had nice families and I was always welcome even though they knew I was different. I counted Chris Verhaegh, Kevin McAleer, Juan Azcarate, Mark Richardson and Bart Devaney among my closest friends. There were others, but these were the few who had actually met and interacted with my mentally defective family, so I figured that if they hadn't run in the opposite direction by now then they probably liked me okay.

Chris was a big hulking kid with long hair parted in the middle and kind of a rebellious guy. My father had a field day teasing him, referring to him as Sasquatch because of his size, or as Chief (from the movie *One Flew Over the Cuckoo's Nest*) due not only to his size but his high cheekbones and the stoic set he had to his face. Chris would always roll with the punch and throw some jazz back my father's way – just enough to keep him honest but not piss him off – and sometimes even make him laugh. No easy trick.

Mark Richardson was a lanky Brit who ran the quarter mile, with big long strides that ate up yardage, a genial guy you couldn't help but like. Kevin and Juan were teammates on both the track and cross-country squads, Juan a handsome Columbian kid who excelled in the middle-distance races. He'd gotten good by running through the coffee fields of his homeland. Kevin was more a surfer than anything and certainly looked the part, with shaggy bleached-blond hair, but also a fine all-around athlete. Not only a good cross-country man but he polevaulted, long-jumped, ran hurdles, anchored our mile-relay team, and later in college he competed in the decathlon. There was almost nothing he couldn't do.

Bart I met through Kevin, and he was a very different guy. Not as guarded as me, with a kind of mischievous leprechaun quality, but at the same time very introspective. Kevin and I would swoop down on Bart's upscale Tarzana home to rifle through his record collection and raid his father's liquor cabinet. One night we three were sitting around drinking and watching Don Kirshner's Rock Concert, a late-night show featuring all the hot acts of the day, and Kevin got so tanked on Jack Daniels whiskey that when he finally had to take a piss he literally rolled off the couch and went on all fours to the bathroom.

"Come on hotshot," taunted Bart. "Go bipedal!"

"It's a new Olympic sport," I laughed. "The 20-meter crawl."

"Let's put a stopwatch on him."

Nothing he couldn't do – except make the bathroom on two legs.

I had to drive him back home to Reseda in his own car. I popped in an eight-track tape he had of the *American Graffiti* soundtrack and we sang oldies all the way to Kevin's place. It had to be close to 2:00 a.m. when we arrived, and as I carried him over my shoulder, wondering how I was going to get him through the front door without waking his parents, Kevin rendered the problem moot by launching into a solo rendition of *The Great Pretender*. The front lights snapped on like we'd been caught in a police-surveillance trap, the door opened, and there stood his mother, one of the nicest people you'd ever hope to meet.

"Hi Mrs. Mac, I think your son has had a bit much to drink."

"Oh dear. Well, thank you for bringing him home, John."

She moved aside as I lugged Kevin through the front door and into his bedroom. I slept on the couch that night and could hear him scurrying to the bathroom at regular intervals to vomit.

At least he was back on his feet.

When my father gained custody of me, I had a forced hiatus from the sports I'd grown to love – football, basketball, baseball. I felt my skillset had diminished, so my confidence level was too low to have any shot at making these teams at Crespi. But I wanted to compete in something so I went out for track and cross country. I figured I could hold my own in middle and long-distance events that required more guts than skill. In cross-country the racing distance was three miles over irregular terrain; in track I ran the half-mile and quarter-mile races as well as the 4x440 relay – and often all three in one meet.

On such days I amended my original thought – not guts but stupidity.

The track team at Crespi was a big deal and there was tremendous pride in its legacy of success. Over the years it had produced several national high-school record holders, two of whom were my teammates in those years. The track program's enduring excellence owed almost entirely to the athletic director and head track coach Bill Leeds. Coach Leeds was extremely demanding and a fairly intimidating figure. He was a big galoot of a guy, his forearms covered by a matting of black hair, and you never caught him wearing any footwear apart from black Riddell coaching shoes and you almost never saw him without an unfiltered Carleton between his lips or fingers. Leeds' practices were very regimented and he had eight assistant coaches watching our every move. Expectations were high and you would be called out by the coaches if they thought you weren't giving one-hundred percent. Each practice we lined up like soldiers in perfect formation and stretched together while the coaches walked through our ranks inspecting us. Not only to make certain everyone stretched properly but also checking for violations of the hair and dress code. After stretching we sat down while Coach Leeds gave some type of inspirational speech or story or just to verbalize some beef he had. He wasn't always pissed off, but certainly most of the time. Then we broke up into our respective disciplines and practice began.

After my sophomore year my father told me I couldn't run track the following year unless I had a job. I told Coach Leeds about my ultimatum; Leeds knew my father was too dangerous to argue with, so I was given a job at school. I worked every day during my free period and the hour between when school ended and practice began. I also worked Saturdays. Mainly dragging the cinder track with heavy iron mesh to smooth it out, cleaning the locker rooms and showers, and doing other odds and ends around the gym. One task involved driving Coach Leeds to and from his apartment before school and after practice. He had me doing everything he could possibly dream up – because at that point I was basically subsidizing my tuition.

So much for my father's investment in my future.

When I was a senior my father surprised me by coming to a track meet. Of the hundreds of athletic events I'd competed in over the years, this was the first time he'd ever showed up to one. I was so nervous that I puked three times. And won a couple races! But of course when I got home he pulled the rug out: "Hey, that's making you sick, you need to get more

75

healthy!" And I'm thinking, oh brother, here we go. It would have been better if he'd never even come.

I competed in track all three years at Crespi, which culminated in my being named co-captain and a High School All-American as a senior.

One of the last events you were required to experience at Crespi Carmelite was a so-called senior retreat. We all went up to some monastery and it involved a lot of self-examination and building up your self-esteem and was basically a three-day love fest. Very touchy-feely. Not really my style, but better than a poke in the eye with a sharp stick. Then came the poke in the eye. It was on the second day and we got a pack of letters telling us how much we were loved and respected and what unique and wonderful individuals we were. The letters were from friends, teachers . . . and family. Those from the parents were READ OUT LOUD. As this nightmare unfolded, one kid after another getting lavish praise and heartfelt words from their parents, I was seriously contemplating a dash for the door. But was also frozen in place. This wasn't happening. Then my letter came. How to describe it? Insincere would be putting it mildly – utter bullshit the more accurate term. I wanted to scream *Stop reading this fiction!* This coming after all the rotten things my father and so-called stepmother had done to me in my life, even right up until I'd left for the retreat, and all of a sudden they'd become lovey-dovey.

You're probably thinking: What other choice did they have? They couldn't just submit a blank sheet of paper or one with big capital letters that said FUCK YOU! But I would have preferred that. At least I could have respected their honesty.

Eight

COLLEGE DAYS

In my senior year of high school I could finally discern the path to breaking away from my family. The plan was to earn my college degree in four years, get a nice paying job, begin working my way up the corporate ladder and never look back. I finished Crespi with an A-minus average and knew that this combined with athletic achievement and a respectable SAT score would get me into a decent university.

I sent applications to a number of California colleges and was accepted at Loyola Marymount University as well as into the UC system. I was considering UCLA and UC Santa Barbara but decided on Loyola because of their business program and owing to the fact that I could live cheaply in the dorms my freshman and sophomore years. In addition it was a Catholic school where many of the kids from the Catholic high-school circuit would be attending. Since my experience at Crespi had been so positive, I naturally gravitated toward a place where I believed the same type of environment would await me.

I was eager to escape from being under my father's roof. My biggest concern was that I knew he would never make my education a priority. Over the years he had pissed away the hundreds of thousands of dollars he'd stolen. If you're going to be a crook then at least hang on to some of your nefarious dough! I lucked out because he had just made a big score and was planning to take the family to Hawaii in the summer of 1979. I passed on the trip and instead asked that he put the money toward my first-semester tuition, which was in the vicinity of four to five thousand dollars. This included room and board in the dorms and would be the one and only time he ever paid the school.

Living in the dorms was fun. Since I had gone to an all-boys high school it was enjoyable finally having girls around. No more restricted contact, no more chaperoned dances on Saturday night with the Catholic girls' schools, now we were all thrown in together, and let's just say it was a boon to my social life.

I adapted easily to college. I knew that initially I would have lots of time on my hands because I wouldn't have to do those chores my father always imposed or spend hours on the overcrowded Los Angeles freeways. Most everything I needed I could find on campus or just a short walk or drive away. I was highly disciplined anyway and could survive on a limited budget. In contrast to other kids. My freshman year was something of an eye-opener since a lot of the other students who lived on campus, many from financially well-off families, would go ape shit partying and taking full advantage of the sudden lack of parental supervision. They had no appreciation of what their parents were spending on their education, and I could see that many of these 18-year-old freshmen would be flunking out by end of the year. I shared their feeling of relief at having escaped the confines of family and home, but after that our attitudes radically diverged. I didn't have the safety net of a family to return to if I failed, so I was loath to take risks – I could ill afford to fuck this up!

I quickly became friendly with other kids and was

reunited with teammates and other pals from Crespi who were attending LMU. Darnell Parker and Rene Lavigne were roommates in the dorm room directly above mine on the first floor. In those days we had eight tracks and cassette tapes and – if you can think back this far – record players. No CDs or other digital stuff with everyone plugged into their own private musical world through their earbuds. And Darnell and Rene seemed not to have discovered the joy of headphones. Unfortunately I failed to share their enthusiasm for the tunes they played – or rather blasted – and on these occasions I would yell my profanity-laced critique of their musical taste up into their window. This led, however, to more amicable encounters. One day Rene asked me if I wanted to play for his intramural flag-football team and I said sure. When I showed up for practice later that afternoon I realized I was the sole white guy on the field and that I'd been recruited by the Black Student Association! This was their freshman team – BSA '83. When I approached them, Rene and Darnell had massive grins on their faces.

"So I guess you need a token white boy," I said.

"That's right," said Rene, "we're backers of affirmative action."

"It's all about promoting diversity," chimed in Darnell.

They were not only good athletes but a fun group to be around. I ended up playing defensive backfield on the team, we won the freshman intramural championship, and I maintained a close friendship with Darnell and Rene as well as teammates Donald Brown and Andre Gueno throughout my four years at LMU.

It was during that Fall of freshman year that a couple upperclassmen visited my dorm to recruit me for the university's crew team. They were targeting high-school athletes and had data detailing my high-school athletic record, which they had apparently accessed through the administrative office. I liked the thought of being out on the water and my imagination had been inspired years before by watching the Olympic rowing as a kid, but from what I knew about rowing it was an elitist Ivy League sport – the polar opposite of most everything I had experienced until now. But like cross-country and middle-distance running, here was another sport I believed I could excel at since the experience factor was not of the highest order, the premium instead being on conditioning and sheer unadulterated guts.

There were some fifty guys trying out for the freshman squad. The first practices were physically demanding and designed to quickly weed people out. By end of the first two weeks only about half of the original fifty remained. Then we started meticulous rowing-technique work on what was called the "barge." The barge had a long rank of rowers on both sides of it and in the middle a narrow catwalk where the coach moved from one rower to the next correcting their technique and if necessary applying the whip. Just kidding, about the whip part. But the barge was something out of a sword-and-sandals epic, primitive in the extreme, though owing to its cumbersome design it was very forgiving of those initial errors committed by novices. One mistake in a sleek expensive racing shell can be catastrophic – not only costing your team a victory but damaging the equipment.

Rowing technique is much harder than you might think. Most people unfamiliar with the sport do not realize you are on a sliding seat and your initial drive is with your legs, then pulling with your back and only then with the arms. Once you complete a stroke you must "release" the oar by pushing downward slightly on the handle while also flicking your left wrist upward (if you're rowing starboard; if you're rowing port then your right wrist performs this action) to flatten or "feather" your oar blade so that it is horizontal to the water as you move back up the sliding seat in preparation for the next "catch." The catch is where you reach the end of your slide, your body now crunched into a tight ball except for your arms which are extended in front of you and the oar blade now squared to the water and you sinking that blade in such a way that it causes "bow splash" – meaning you cause water to splash backward toward the bow. Or rather forward toward the bow. Remember you're going backward this whole time, the coxswain in the stern of the boat and keeping it straight down the course.

It is when all these component aspects of the stroke are in perfect sync that "swing" occurs. When all eight rowers are completely attuned to one another, at every catch you can feel the shell lift from the water and it rushing under the hull. It's a weightless and seamless feeling. Even when you're in the middle of a race and think that with the very next stroke you're going to pass out, the feeling of swing can revive you. Athletes speak of being "in the zone," and maybe it's something similar, only with rowing there's the group aspect, which makes that perfectly calibrated feeling particularly hard to come by since all eight rowers have to be in the zone at once.

Needless to say, as a freshman rower swing was pretty hard to come by. Our freshman coach was a complete maniac named Brad Owen. After double sessions, otherwise known as hell week, we began referring to him as Rad Brad. It was Brad's first year coaching and he used the freshmen oarsmen as his guinea pigs. Here it should be said that Fall season was short and usually entailed one long three-mile race, then taking a couple months off before the spring racing season, sometimes referred to as sprint season, where the races were 2000 meters, roughly a mile and a quarter. But whether the

Fall or sprint season, Rad Brad would have us row long distances of four, six or eight miles. These long pieces are rough on the hands, and many of us learned the hard way to trim calluses when they got too thick; during a long piece you could feel blood blisters forming between the thick calluses. In the course of these pieces a blister would both form and then pop, the blood dripping from your oar handle and the stinging salt water entering the wound.

Brad also liked to play mind games. Through his megaphone, sitting in the launch, he would inform us that we'd be rowing our last piece of the practice, which was always a welcome announcement – but after the piece he would then declare himself unhappy with our performance and to sit ready for an eight miler! He did this enough times that guys began flipping out. One time a kid started screaming that he wouldn't row another fucking stroke and then unlaced himself from his shoes and dove over the side of the racing shell and started swimming to the dock. We got him calmed down and back in the boat.

The varsity guys screwed with the freshman, performing practical jokes and indulging in other ball-breaking activity, but it was mostly in good fun. I say "mostly" because these guys were serious about winning and wanted to instill that attitude in us. Crew at LMU was a big deal and the program had a proud tradition which the upperclassman made certain you were aware of. Our freshman team had a decent season that year but not spectacular. One thing was sure though – I'd caught the rowing bug.

I was excited to start my sophomore year but full of stress and anxiety. I'd earned a few bucks working on my uncles' roofing companies in Chicago that summer, but not nearly enough to cover college tuition and other expenses. I knew my father wasn't going to spend another dime on my education. He had other priorities. Like fancy cars, houses and cosmetic surgery for his annoying wife. So, achieving financial clearance to enroll each semester was a war of nerves. Second semester of my freshman year my father had given me a bum check – but thankfully it only bounced after I'd been enrolled and was already attending class. I found this out when I reached the front of the line attempting to enroll for my sophomore year. I had no money but told them my father would take care of it soon and they gave me a pass.

While in Chicago over the summer, I had competed in a boxing tournament and had really become fired-up on the sport, so I brought most of my equipment including a speed bag to my dorm when I moved back. I was intent on installing the speed bag in my dorm room but wasn't sure it was allowed – of course I did it anyway figuring the worst the Resident Advisor could do was make me take it down. The walls in the dorm were thick with mason block so I borrowed an old nail gun to install the speed-bag frame. This nail gun required that you line up a thin steel plate between the nail and the wall to prevent the nail from going all the way through the wall. Additionally, also for safety reasons, you had to apply forward pressure to trigger the gun. Trying to balance the frame, the gun and the plate while applying forward pressure was tricky, and the steel plate slipped out just at the moment when I pulled the trigger – sending the nail all the way through the wall and into the adjacent dorm room. I went over and knocked on the door thinking I might have killed my neighbor. Great. All I needed. But since I had moved in a week early – members of the crew team were allowed early access to the dorms because our intensive training started a week before classes went into session – there were no occupants, dead or otherwise, in the adjacent room. It was through the help of a fellow oarsman that I finally got the bag up. Not only could I keep my timing honed but there was an unexpected side-benefit. Anytime anyone was partying or playing music too loudly, all I had to do was get on the speed bag. The acoustics in the dorms were such that when I went full bore on the bag it thundered down the hallway. If the miscreants were just the other side of the wall then the vibration could even cause a record to skip and scratch.

Another result of the speed bag was that word got around and a number of guys asked me to teach them boxing, which I did in the recreation room on the top floor of the dorms. It was a mild version of *Fight Club* because after teaching some of my dorm-mates the basics, I'd have them strap on the gloves and go at it. I kept it under control and never allowed anyone to be brutalized, but bloody noses and black eyes were inevitable. And to some degree the point. These guys wanted to mix it up. Next thing I knew we were a feature-article in the school paper, which made administrators aware of what we were doing and they forced us to shut down. Since I worked out constantly at the gym, I would often run into the LMU men's athletic director, Robert Arias, who was equally fanatical about staying fit. We often exchanged conversation and he became something of an ally, secretly helping to fund my now underground boxing program. He believed as I did that the administration was overreacting. He slipped me some funds from his budget to purchase better headgear and other equipment. No way such a thing could happen in this day and age when administrators are scared shitless of lawsuits about the slightest mickey-mouse stuff – and here we were banging each other around without official sanction.

Three cheers for Robert Arias – a man with real cojones!

As a sophomore you were free to join a fraternity, which I had no interest in doing. However, during "rush" week when the fraternities had all kinds of events in order to recruit candidates, I took advantage by attending these functions to score free food and drink. Being on a shoe-string budget, freeloading on fraternity events was a semi-necessity for me to get by. I was pretty open with the frat brothers as to what I was doing and they didn't seem to care.

Or maybe my "fight club" reputation helped, I don't know.

That sophomore year I became a member of the varsity rowing squad, whose coach was John Trigilio – Trig for short. I really liked Trig. He was experienced and seemed much more balanced than Rad Brad. Several of the freshmen rowers from the year before decided not to row again, so our talent pool was limited. We had a rough season up until our last couple races when things finally started to jell. Our season finale was the Western Sprints, which is the last major regatta on the west coast and this year was being held in the Navy Shipyard in Vallejo, California, near San Francisco. LMU provided a luxury bus for the eight-hour ride up to the Bay Area. We did well enough in our heat to make the final in which eight teams were competing. Many if not all of these squads had crushed us during the season, yet we ended up taking the silver and were surging as the race ended. We then took half the oarsmen from our eight, me included, and won the four with cox – whom we promptly tossed in the drink. Another crew tradition is that the vanquished teams come and surrender their jerseys to the victor. With these surrogate scalps in hand we headed for home – but not before directing our bus driver to stop at a liquor store – and we drank and sang all the way back to LMU.

The summer of 1981, I spent about a month in Chicago and then a few weeks at my father's sizeable ranch house in Camarillo. It was a memorable return home as I walked directly into a family brawl. Apparently my older sister and younger brother were in some type of trouble that had caused my father to go on a rampage. He was in the process of beating them down when I walked in and was met with a pool cue directly across the forehead. I remember seeing stars and going down on one knee. I tried to shake it off but the moment I attempted to stand I felt nauseous, so I stayed on one knee until the cobwebs and nausea cleared. Welcome home to reality college boy! The lump on my head and the nausea lasted a few days, another penny being added to the already full jar of disgust I'd stored up for my father, and in those few days I was also able to confirm that he would not be paying another penny toward my tuition. Yet here he was living in a close to million-dollar home with a tennis court, pool, some horses and a stretch limo in the large circular driveway – all assets that had been either directly or indirectly conned from someone. Although I knew this was likely a losing battle, in a last-ditch effort to get my father to make my tuition a priority, I detailed my accomplishments in school including my B+ average and the fact that I had made the varsity rowing team. Big mistake. He couldn't wait to get on the phone with my aunts and uncles and tell them that his son was the "head stroke" at school. Since these simpletons had no clue as to what a crew team even was, they all had a nice laugh at my expense. Within hours of overhearing this conversation I blasted out of that asylum and stayed at the homes of two of my old friends, Kevin McAleer and Juan Azcarate, until I was able to move back to the LMU campus. I was more than usually excited about the coming year since not only Kevin but high-school pal Bart Devaney had enrolled at LMU. Bart had transferred from Villanova and Kevin came by way of Cal State Northridge where he'd been doing the ten-eventer. Since Loyola didn't have a track & field program, he was now aiming for the crew team, and we'd started training together that summer.

As a junior I was no longer allowed to live in the dorms and so I moved into an on-campus apartment with three other guys. This gave me a place to stay without having to pay the necessary fees – though somehow financial clearance was again miraculously granted. Was my old man pulling off another one of his master scams? That was probably giving him too much credit. He didn't care if I spent another day at college. In any event I made no further inquiries, just feeling lucky and hoping my luck would hold.

On the downside, however, and to the aggravation of returning varsity oarsmen, our new coach my junior year was Mike Priest. A man nearly all the guys despised. He had been exclusively the women's coach in previous years, but due to budget cuts this year the men's varsity would also be under his auspices. Our first day of practice we were greeted by a locked shell house – our place in Marina del Rey where all the equipment was stored and where we launched our racing shells for practice – and with a big sign telling us that our new varsity coach was on strike!

This set the tone for the next two years.

We had the talent to become a top boat that season. Joe Early was our stroke man and sat in the eight seat, facing the coxswain. The eight man, or stroke man, is typically your best and most experienced oarsman and Early had the perfect rower's physique. Tall with long arms and an absolute minimum of body fat, muscles and veins so close to the skin that he looked like a walking anatomy chart. The other two seniors were Russ Schatz and Alex Barretto. Both very strong and experienced oarsmen, particularly Russ. They sat mostly in the five and six seats respectively, known as the engine room, and Russ and Alex were also inseparable off the water. They were always pulling pranks. For instance Barretto would engage a guy in close conversation, preferably with women's crew members present, and then Russ would come from behind and yank down his shorts. That was a favorite of theirs. I think we all got the treatment one time or another. In any event we had a great season, winning most of our dual meets and always finishing in the top three at major regattas. Unfortunately for us the University of Santa Clara had an extremely fast crew that year and ended up winning the West Coast Championships; we took bronze.

Junior year I established myself as a team leader and was elected by popular vote to become next season's Commodore, the de facto captain of the men's varsity squad. This also entailed being president of the Loyola Rowing Association (LRA), a fraternal organization of rowers which included alumni. I was given a key to the shellhouse and my voice was the decisive one when it came to most if not all those activities where Coach Priest was not directly involved. The LRA had a budget of a few thousand dollars used to sponsor certain events during the year, including the one-night initiation of new LRA members and the "Curfew Party," which was one of the school's hot tips because of its exclusivity and location. Our shellhouse was literally on the water in Marina Del Rey – wakes from passing boats would make the floating shellhouse gently rise and fall – and so it constituted great atmosphere for a bash. One wall was a big picture window, and you could take a spiral staircase and go up top to get an even more panoramic view of the marina. But as fun as it was, the Curfew Party also signaled the start of serious training.

A few words on that. The races stay less in memory than the training and practices. Because they were tougher. On race days you had the nervous energy to get you through 2000 meters, but in a six-practice or even twelve-practice week you had neither the adrenalin nor the charged atmosphere to attenuate the pain. Crew was a savage regime, combining the endurance of a distance runner with explosive strength. In boxing you could maybe coast through a round and every three minutes you had a breather on your stool, but in crew there were no breathers. It was relentless. I remember roadwork each morning, running up a steep 180-foot hill of sand – or trying to – basically slogging up it for thirty yards and semi-crawling for the second half and by the fifteenth time on your hands and knees, and thousands of jump-squats and bang-the-boards – where you lie face-down on a bench and hoist a barbell till it smacks the underside of the bench – and pull-ups and laps in the pool and grueling sessions on the ergometer and it was only then that you got to the rowing. That's what I remember most – the training.

Toward the end of my junior year I got a call from my good friend Miguel Flores. I had first made Miguel's acquaintance in the boxing ring, squaring off with him in an exhibition bout at a gym in North Chicago called Degerberg Academy in the summer of 1978. Every year since our exhibition we would stage a rematch either in Chicago or LA depending on who was visiting whom. It was great when Mike came out because he'd bring a wad of cash and we'd eat and drink at nice places. Sometimes we'd hit the local dives and college bars where I had the supreme task of keeping Miguel from hurting someone. I wasn't always successful. One time we were at a local place called "Jack's" and playing pool. Some wannabe tough guy mouthed off to Miguel who replied with a beautiful right cross – not beautiful for the victim, of course, since he wound up unconscious on the floor.

"All right," I said, "let's blow this taco stand."

"No way – we gotta finish our game."

Miguel had just taken out their "heavy," so their confidence was destroyed, but you never knew in these situations. And I'd already had an earlier encounter with a wayward cue stick and wasn't eager for another.

"You moron, this isn't Chicago, they might call the cops!"

I hustled him out but almost as soon as we hit the alley behind the bar he wanted to head back in.

"Hey Johnny, I can't leave like that. Those jerk-offs probably think we're afraid. I'm going in for one last drink."

"You've had enough."

"Just one for the road."

"One for the road nothin'! Get your drunken ass in the car!"

"Easy Johnny, don't talk to me that way."

"I'll talk to you any fucking way I want."

"Oh no you won't."

He took a swing at me. A left hook this time. I caught it on my right forearm, threw a left of my own, and a second later we'd hit the asphalt and were rolling around getting cut up on the alley glass and other sharp-edged debris. This was ridiculous. Finally, as if by silent consensus, we both got to our feet.

"I'm out of here," I said. "If you want to come with, you're welcome, if not then find your own way home."

I walked to my car. He wasn't following. I got in and started the engine. I'd just shifted into first and was pulling out into the street when I heard a THUMP on my roof and saw Miguel's upside-down face grinning maniacally through the windshield. I kept driving. I was in no mood to tangle with this madman again. We were only a few blocks from campus so I drove slowly with Miguel spread-eagled on the roof. His elbow was bloodied from our wrestling so he decided to use his arm as a windshield wiper spreading blood across the glass. I was longing for the days when I only had to carry inebriated friends into their houses. We finally pulled up to the campus security booth. The guard came out.

"Hey there's a drunk guy on your roof."

"No shit."

Miguel later became a standard-bearer for law and order as a policeman in Chicago's 13th district.

Hanging with my sparring partner Miguel made me want to get a couple fights in that summer. I met Ray Notaro at the Left Hook Gym in the west San Fernando Valley and he invited me to train there. Ray had trained Sylvester Stallone for the movie *Rocky*. Unfortunately the drive from LMU was too far. But I ended up getting a couple fights, all right, though neither of them in the ring. The first happened playing pick-up basketball with my college pal Jim Reiss at a park not far from LMU. Jim was on the rugby team and we were always busting each other's chops over our respective sports. He'd say crew was eight guys sitting on their ass going backward with some midget screaming at them, I'd come back with something equally uncomplimentary, so basketball was neutral territory. There were many regulars playing at this park, a predominantly black crowd, and there was lots of trash talk but all in good fun.

This one day Jim and I ended up on a decent team and had won four straight games when some guys we didn't recognize showed up. Two or three of them were wearing Hertz T-shirts, and since we were close to the airport I presumed they worked there. For our game they were shirts and we were skins. They were talking trash right out of the gate and almost the second I touched the ball for the first time the apparent ringleader of the Hertz gang yelled out "Travelin'!" Nonsense. I hadn't walked with the ball. And even if I had, I was backcourt on a stupid inbound pass. I kept dribbling up court. Then once more – "Travelin', end of argument" – and he tried wrestling the ball from my hands. The guy was built like a fullback and had these dangly cornrow thingies hanging from his scalp – kind of like that character from the old *Our Gang* comedy shorts.

"Fuck you Buckwheat!" I said as he kept trying to grab the ball.

The comment caused laughter even among the black dudes on his team – but a reserved kind of chuckle like *You gonna take that from whitey?* By this point the ball was bouncing free and we'd each taken a couple steps back – as one does when squaring off with a potential opponent. Buckwheat charged. And in the most bizarre way. He lowered his head with his arm extended in a fist. I was surprised by this unorthodox attack. His extended fist caught me on my forehead just as I managed stepping to the side of this human projectile and firing a right hand which caught him on the top of his head and left me with a cut on my knuckles. From the guy's weirded-out hair! With my left arm I got him in a headlock as he used his momentum to try and pile-drive me into the concrete. My feet were moving backward fast while I tried to guide myself into the thick steel pole holding up the backboard. Luckily I hit it and was able to slide down to my seat with Buckwheat still in a headlock. Now he's slamming his body into me like a football player would with a blocking sled. I get my right arm under his left armpit and manage to turn him on his back. As I make this move my left knee ends up on his right shoulder with his head pushed up against the steel pole and I hear this loud disturbing pop. The pole had prevented the rest of his body from following as his shoulder gave way and so it popped out of the socket. He was screaming in agony. A pretty nasty injury.

"That's what you get Buckwheat motherfucker!"

This was me again. Standing over him. Then I looked up and saw a sizeable crowd gathered. I thought for sure his

Hertz friends were going to jump me but instead they just picked him up and took him away, likely to a hospital.

"Let's get the fuck outta here!"

That was Jim.

We did as he suggested.

Driving away in his old Mustang I assessed the damage. Both hands cut up, a lump on the front and back of my head, my spine feeling like it'd been rammed against a steel pole which it had.

"Buckwheat," said Jim. "That's what you come up with when we're the only white guys at the fucking park?"

"Tell me he *didn't* look like Buckwheat."

No more than a week later I'm out again with Jim. This time in Marina Del Rey at a restaurant called The Red Onion, which had a nightclub downstairs called "Pearl Harbor."

Very poetic.

Since a sneak attack was in the offing.

After a few beers Jim and I headed back to campus, and as I'm leaving the parking lot in my Oldsmobile, a car in front of me stops suddenly and I hit the brakes. Two girls and two guys heading toward The Red Onion entrance now have to stop because my car is blocking their path. Before walking around my car one of them kicks it. I look at Jim and put the car in park and get out to survey any damage, of which there was none, and one of the women in the foursome starts screaming at me. I ignore her and climb back in the car.

Now I know this sounds slightly out of character. In most circumstances I would at very least have torn into them verbally and no way kept quiet in the face of some hysterical shrieking bitch. But mind you I was coming off the fight with Buckwheat where I could have gotten deep-sixed with a knife between the ribs. Those brothers didn't fool around. So maybe not turning over a new leaf, but leastwise giving it a rest. Then I hear a guy's voice blurt out:

"You *better* get back in that car asshole!"

I look at Jim. This can't be happening. He just says:

"Kill 'em."

Not that I'm going to. But I get out and take a few steps toward them. This is very irritating. Here I am trying to exercise restraint for once in my life and these jerk-offs won't give me a fighting chance.

"What did you say?"

It's almost nice the way I ask it. And no name-calling or other profanities. I'm feeling pretty proud of myself. But now the big mouth comes toward me with balled fists at his side and head shoved forward and snarls:

"I'm going to kick your ass."

Jeezus. Where does this guy get his dialogue? That and his posture tells me it's amateur hour. He's too pathetic to punch. I don't even bother assuming a fighting stance. I just stand sideways waiting for this imbecile to get into range. Otherwise I'm keeping my fists to myself. But the guy is insistent. Probably since the girls are watching. The poor bastard. Don't do it, keep off me, it's not worth it, believe me pal . . .

A straight right. Perfectly timed. And square on the bridge of his nose. Again a popping sound. But this one more familiar. It's that sound you hear in the gym when a fighter busts his nose for the first time, commonly referred to as getting his "cherry broke." But this is almost laughable. He hits the deck and is holding his face as both eyes well up with tears. Jim jumps from the car but the other guy wants no part of the ruckus. At least one of them with some brains. He kneels on the ground tending to his friend. But it's not over yet. One of the women runs up, the screaming Mimi of before, and tries to punch me in the face. I fend her off but then the other woman jumps in and starts punching and scratching me. In the midst of this onslaught I fall over a curb and Mimi sits on my chest and starts swinging wildly while the other has fun gouging my cheeks. But Mimi is light so I toss her off and regain my feet but then both are after me again and I have all I can do to fend off their punches. Where the hell's Jim? He's off to one side laughing is where he is. He calls over:

"I'm keeping an eye on the other two!"

I finally grab Mimi by the wrists and twist them hard enough to put her on her knees while telling the other one I'll break her arm if she doesn't back off.

"Let me go!" says Mimi.

"Let her go!" says her friend.

"First you stop punching and scratching me!"

They both leave off.

I let go.

They both start punching me again.

Finally I understand – if that guy hadn't threatened to kick my ass then they would have kicked *his* ass. Now the doormen come out to see me fighting these two banshees:

"Hey we're gonna call the cops!"

"Please do!" I yell back.

The two women relent. They go back to their beta males. Jim and I jump into my car, its motor still running, and I pull out of the parking lot.

"I'm starting to see a trend here," I say – "Anytime I'm with you there's trouble."

"Oh sure," he says, "Like you need me around to get into a fight."

This time yes. I looked at my face in the rearview mirror. Deep gouges with blood tricking down my face and my hands and forearms full of scratches. This was going to be hard to explain back at school – injuries obviously incurred by a woman's fingernails – the type injuries inflicted on an unsuccessful rapist – now I'll have to tell this ridiculous story a hundred times . . .

That summer, when I wasn't taking shots from girls, I was taking my duties as LRA Commodore very seriously. For instance I solicited members of the men's team to work on the shellhouse and some of the highly degradable equipment stored there, including the training barge and the varsity racing shells, replacing their slides, oarlocks and seats as well as sanding and varnishing their hulls. We had them in tip-top shape and were banking on their performance. Not only did we have returning varsity rowers Jim Drake, Kevin McAleer and myself but there were strong oarsman coming up from the freshman and JV teams, so we were anticipating a banner year.

However this excitement was offset by extreme anxiety because my debt had grown to over 40K. How would I ever be given financial clearance to register for my senior year? I was desperate enough to appeal to both sides of my family. Unfortunately my mother's side was in no position to help. On my father's side – crickets. With the exception of one pleasant surprise. My paternal grandmother, the crazy lady, sent me a check for a thousand dollars, which wasn't going to get me clearance, but it did help get me by on a day- to –day basis.

I was naturally grateful but also considered it my just due for all those times I had beaten up or threatened her imagined enemies.

On registration day, when I finally reached the front of the line, they pulled my file and saw the five-digit debt and immediately directed me to the office of university president Father Donald Merrifield SJM. I had met Father Merrifield on previous occasions and knew him to be a very nice person, but that didn't mitigate my nervousness as I took a deep breath and knocked on his office door. I heard a voice telling me to come in and when I pushed open the door he said he'd been expecting me.

I imagine owing forty large and entering my final semester had a little something to do with him expecting me.

I took a seat and we began to converse. He seemed to know a lot about me, my GPA, that I'd been voted captain of the rowing team. He even noted my having played intramural football for the Black Student Association. He knew my entire high school academic and athletic record. Then came the topper – he casually mentioned that he had spoken with my father. My heart sank imagining how that conversation went down. I figured I was doomed. I was just waiting for Merrifield to call security and have me escorted off campus. But instead he stated that he was going to help me finish school. He gave me the folder with my records and directed me to the head of the finance office. I stammered my thanks – something to the effect of the weight of the world being lifted from my shoulders – and at the finance office my clearance papers were signed by another understanding fellow who smiled and said, "What's another few grand when you already owe forty!" Then it was on to the financial-aid office where I filed for grants, student loans and a work-study job on campus.

I'd caught a break due to the compassion of Father Donald Merrifield SJM.

Though I still wonder what might have been said in that conversation he had with my father.

I wonder because a short while later when I asked my father about it he gave me one of his typical in-your-face replies: "You don't know and don't wanna know!" This was on occasion of me telephoning to hit him up for a C-note to buy books for my final semester. I thought it would be an opportune moment because now he had an office at Sunset & Gower Studios, which his present financial prosperity apparently allowed for. He told me to come by the next day to visit him and when I arrived he was with a couple of his crew, Jimmy Lucas and Roberto Mayo.

Jimmy was a slick-talking Greek and my father's accomplice in many of his past capers. Roberto was a big intimidating Spaniard, a well-known loan shark and feared collector of bad debts. He was an ex-boxer who had fought under the moniker "Irish Billy Williams." His claim to fame was having fought Chuck Wepner in 1974 – Wepner one of only three men to have put Muhammed Ali on the canvas. I greeted everyone. They all seemed in an exceptionally good mood, smiling and laughing.

"So Pop," I said after more small talk, "what about the hundred dollars? Like I said, I need it for books." I never called him "Pop" but his mood and my desire to soften him up elicited it.

I expected some crack along the lines of what a fucking waste of money or some other imbecile comment but instead he just grinned and said no problem – though I had to get it from his friend Roy who had just crossed the street to the deli to pick up lunch for the group. Roy was holding the money in case the three of them had to leave the office before I got there.

I had met Roy only once. He was a black guy my height but much bulkier. I didn't want to wait around for his return so I crossed the street and caught him just as he was exiting the deli.

"Hey Roy," I said sticking out my hand. "I don't know if you remember me but I'm Mario's kid."

He didn't take my hand, just looked at me crosswise and puffed out his beefy chest: "I don't give a fuck who you are punk."

Huh? The guy's response was so obnoxious that I didn't

even think but just reacted, grabbing his throat and pushing him up against the storefront window, which shook hard, all the people inside turning their heads in our direction.

"Alright motherfucker, you wanna fucking start with me?"

With my left hand still on his neck, I had my right raised and ready to drill him. He had been unprepared for the intensity of my response – probably because I myself had been unprepared for it. I rarely snapped that quickly.

"No, no," shaking his head, "be cool, be cool. Your father told me to do this. He said you would take it as a joke."

Of course. After all these years my father was still testing me. I released my grip.

"Sorry man," I said. "He's probably looking out the window right now and laughing his ass off."

"Least someone is."

I explained my errand and Roy peeled off a C-note and handed it to me. It could have been just that simple – but my father had to make a twisted game of everything.

In recalling my final semester at LMU there are several events etched in my mind. Outside of the increased intensity of our training, the 1983 season included both big wins and bitter losses. But more challenging than the physical rigors of rowing was getting along with our coach. Toward end of the fall season and prior to starting my final semester, our team participated in a couple television shows. There was "That's Incredible" which typically featured some type of oddball talent or stunt. In this case it involved a number of west-coast collegiate rowing teams pulling a water skier behind them in a race. Although there were a couple people in our rowing program who were lighter and more experienced water skiers than our coach, he decided that he was the man for the job. As suspected, within the first few hundred meters, with us near or in the lead, he went down and we came in last. Our appearance on the Jack LaLanne show was a lot more fun. For those of you who might not remember, Jack LaLanne was a fitness icon who was known for performing extraordinary feats of strength and conditioning – like swimming the length of the Golden Gate Bridge underwater while handcuffed, shackled and pulling a thousand pound boat when he was over 60 years old. Insane stuff like that. He must have been about 70 when myself and three teammates appeared on the show to stretch and exercise with him and his wife Elaine LaLanne. Beat that for a name. After the show we took turns punching him in the gut, which was hard as granite. As we left the studio, Jack called after us – "Fitness is king and nutrition is queen – put them together and you've got a kingdom!"

A real original, Jack LaLanne.

This was followed by the first stunt at LMU where my Chicago street savvy kicked in. As the LRA Commodore, I was entitled to put forward nominees for Homecoming King and Queen. This wasn't something the LRA necessarily did every year; it was simply an option, and one rarely exercised, mostly because the fraternities and sororities had a lock on the thing. What was the use? Like a Californian voting for the Republican presidential candidate. But I was determined to break the fraternity stranglehold. First I approached my friend and teammate Kevin McAleer and asked if he might be interested.

"I hate that gay shit," he said. "It's for frat boys and assholes."

"That's the point," I said. "We're going to hand them their lunch this year."

"How you gonna do that?"

"Just trust me."

"And why me anyhow?"

"Cuz you're the only one with any hair!"

The week before, after a crushing loss to one of the San Diego schools, we had done group penance by shaving our heads. This was typical crew stuff. It was supposed to be a gesture of solidarity and commitment, but at its root lay the idea that now you *had* to win or look like a bunch of weenies. Kevin didn't shave his head though. The sole exception. He could be obdurate that way. But now I was using his obduracy to my own purposes and he finally consented – probably *because* he hadn't shaved his head and felt he owed the team a little self-sacrifice now.

In the past there had always been foul play with fraternities stuffing the ballot box, but who knows better how to fix an election than someone from Chicago? Most people know that if it weren't for Sam Giancana and the first Mayor Daley, a Roman Catholic like JFK would never have carried Illinois and eventually the country. This Homecoming election would come down to who was more cunning, me or some silver-spoon frat punks.

The first thing we wanted to do was make a joke of the entire deal – just throwing the whole thing back in their teeth – so Kev and I selected one of the stupidest photos possible of him. While all the frat candidates had perfect shots of themselves in suit and tie, not a hair out of place, Kevin's official photo was of him doing some goofball dance in his grimy surf trunks and blond hair flying around. Totally undignified. Next thing was to not even bother stuffing the ballot box. Way too predictable! And iffy. Maybe you get outstuffed. Instead I went directly to the guy responsible for counting the ballots, the head of the Associated Students, whom I knew slightly, and just used simple reason. I told him that we all knew the frat boys had the elections rigged from the get-go – stuffing the ballot box and recruiting voters and otherwise mustering whatever influence they could bring to bear – and then I posed two simple questions. 1) If there was going to be cheating anyway, why couldn't someone else get the nod for a change? 2) Would he rather face me or some yuppie-larva frat boy if our respective candidates didn't win?

The Homecoming game was in the Albert Gerston Pavilion and at half-time of the basketball game they would be announcing the king and queen. Getting Kevin to don one of my dress jackets was a struggle, though he finally did, but he flatly refused to wear a tie.

"You're gonna win, Kev, you gotta look good for this."

"So I win. But murder me, cut my balls off, I'm not wearing any tie."

A man has his standards.

So here was this scruffy surf rat standing mid-court with the other half dozen candidates, all well-scrubbed and decked out in their sartorial best, the stands are packed and they start announcing the runners-up, and finally it's just Kevin and this Sigma Pi dipshit. Mr. Sigma Pi is standing ramrod straight, a smug look on his face, waiting to receive his due honor while Kev is just slouched, hands shoved in his pockets, a derisive sneer on his lips. Who is this derelict? Apart from the crew guys, nobody in the school knows him. *Everyone* knows Mr. Sigma Pi. The girls in the bleachers are screaming, they can hardly stand it.

"And the 1983 Loyola Marymount Homecoming King is . . . KEVIN MCALEER!"

Kev's sneer altered slightly to a smirk, but you should have seen Sigma Pi's face. I believe the word is "crestfallen." How can they do this to me? It's MY crown – MINE!

Boo hoo.

Then they announced the Homecoming Queen, who was a sorority sister, which was a nice capper.

How come SHE wins and we DON'T?

Our crew team was winning, all right. We had a fast boat and gained the reputation of "giant killers" since we were beating the larger schools with their far greater talent pool. We took first place in the Newport Regatta and were nudged out of gold in the West Coast championships by seven-tenths of a second. Heartbreaking. But we rallied and put together a four-man squad to win the U.S. Southwest Regionals.

Then came the season-ending awards banquet. As indicated, I wasn't on the best of terms with Coach Priest. We'd had a number of confrontations during the season. There was the time he put the women's novice crew into a racing shell reserved for the men's varsity and they crashed it into the rocks near the breakwater; the time he got drunk on Saint Patrick's Day and canceled practice; the time he tried to screw me over by having a special team vote for captaincy of the squad, though the Commodore had traditionally held that title – a fact underscored by the team when they affirmed me as captain in Priest's self-willed election. I was a bit self-willed myself, and I'll grant that Priest had great know-how when it came to the finer points of rowing and rigging a boat (for instance he installed a "bucket rig" so that I as a starboard rower could be in the stroke seat) but our respective styles simply failed to mesh. This personality conflict came to a head at the awards banquet when Priest pulled some dipsy-doodle to deny me any awards. Traditionally the Leadership Award was voted by the men's varsity, but this year no vote was taken and Priest decided that he himself would select the honoree, which needless to say wasn't yours truly. Then he reconceived the Outstanding Oarsman award to delineate not rowing ability but "improvement" and "effort." Or something. No one in our varsity eight was deemed good enough by these criteria, the award going to a rower previously bumped from the varsity to the JV squad. It was an utterly transparent dodge.

I gave the speech I'd prepared as Commodore, restraining myself from any angry interpolations, then immediately left the banquet with Kevin at my side. We took a long walk around the marina.

"I guess that was one election you couldn't rig."

"Priest hates my guts."

"You know, if he was going to give that award to someone who didn't deserve it, he could at least have given it to *me*."

Kev was proud of the fact that he was a shitty rower since it bespoke his matchless power – the only reason he was in the varsity boat. Usually your bowman was the best technical rower on the team, but we theorized that Priest's rationale for putting Kevin at bow was to be away from the rest of the rowers and thereby minimizing the damage he could do. If true it would have been an interesting twist on the received wisdom – and typical of Priest's sometimes unfathomable actions.

All graduating oarsmen got a nine-inch length of varnished wood oar with "LMU CREW 1983" embossed on it, and now I reared back and flung mine into the marina.

But there was more behind that gesture than just my contempt for Priest. I'd sent out invitations to my family for not only the banquet but my upcoming graduation and hadn't received a single response. Then again, in four years no member of my family had attended a single crew race, so why break with tradition? Combined with my disappointment from the crew event, I elected to distance myself from the graduation ceremony. I probably wouldn't have picked up a diploma anyway, since my father hadn't paid three and a half years of back-tuition. From both a sporting and academic perspective, it almost seemed as if those four college years had never happened.

Nine

That summer I interviewed at a number of large and small firms. What I found most interesting about the interview process is how most companies seemed far more interested in my high-school and college sports record than my GPA, major or any classes I'd completed. Obviously the American corporate world was looking for ambitious performers and not retiring scholars. But my entire life I had only ever worked blue-collar jobs – as a groundskeeper, gas-station attendant, usher in a movie theater, as my father's roofing laborer and accomplice –so wearing a suit and tie everyday would be a new experience. I received three offers, two with large financial firms, and finally accepted a job at a small semiconductor-processing company specializing in military, space and medical markets. It was the 1980s and business was booming as President Ronald Reagan presided over a renewed arms build-up. Unlike today, in the 1980s the U.S. Department of Defense was the force that drove the demand for microelectronics.

I moved into a nice condo in Playa Del Rey, not far from my alma mater and right near the beach. I had a few roommates, all college guys from LMU. It was a twenty-minute drive to the office. Although Marina Del Rey was right nearby, I left the sport of rowing behind since I now had a strong desire to resume boxing. Within weeks of settling into my job as an inside-sales/customer-service rep, I found a boxing gym and started training.

I made friends at work fairly easily. My stepbrother – the first son of my father's second wife from a previous marriage – worked at this company and he made certain to introduce me around. Over the years he and I had had our differences and several fistfights but we always made up and eventually got to like and respect each other. Like most everyone else, I called him "Sinbad" – as in Sinbad the Sailor since he was a U.S. Navy veteran. He had a muscular torso like a bodybuilder and was a couple years older than me, but this of course never stopped me from mixing it up with him. I would take a few shots as long as I could deliver one good blow upside his head. However, as Sinbad witnessed me becoming stronger and my fighting skills more polished, he was no longer so anxious to fight me.

I performed well at work and within a year was promoted to Program Manager, a very stressful and difficult job. Each specific program required that you undergo advanced testing, and to qualify for a given task was challenging. Everything boiled down to statistics, and quality was paramount because it's nearly impossible to fix a malfunctioning device on a satellite or other space vehicle once it has been launched. For manned spaceflight missions the safety of the astronaut is of chief concern, and failure of a weapons system can cause death of the operator and other collateral damage. There was also the issue of getting the ordered merchandise delivered to our customer on time. This could sometimes mean millions of dollars in early-delivery incentive clauses when it came to certain top-secret programs.

That first year I gained tremendous knowledge in the

qualifying process of high-reliability semiconductors and integrated circuits. Seeing the process up close gave me a clear understanding of what each test was designed to do and why. Reading and comprehending complex military, space and customer specifications certainly helped me gain promotions, but I believe the key factor was having a great relationship with the grinders on the production floor. These were workers who typically despised white-collar sales guys. My blue-collar attitude and roots enabled me to effectively communicate with these line workers and I often played basketball with them. They also loved the fact that I was still competing in boxing. Almost every day after work I would drive down to Joe Louis Memorial Gym in Santa Monica. At first I just kept to myself, working out and observing the trainers. I wanted to see how they were bringing along some of the other fighters in the gym. That's when I met LC Morgan. He was 50 years old, a charming man with an infectious smile. His face reminded me of Redd Foxx from the TV series *Sanford and Son*. LC was the most experienced boxer I ever met, having had nearly 140 fights as a welterweight. He agreed to train me. He would always get in his stance and rock back and forth throwing out stiff jabs and saying: "Johnny you gotta be like a crocodile!"

I was leaving the gym one Saturday morning when I saw a Rolls Royce pull up and Bundini Brown, sidekick to Muhammed Ali, exit the car and open the back door and then out stepped the champ himself. I followed Ali back into the gym. Whatever I had planned for that afternoon could wait. Soon a camera crew was setting up in the gym and Ali emerged from the dressing room in workout gear. Since it was a Saturday morning, not many fighters were present and I found a great seat on the ring apron just outside the ropes and watched as Ali moved around the ring shadowboxing. He was something to behold. A man 6'3", probably 240 pounds at the time, over forty years old and moving around the ring like a fast young middleweight. His speed and agility were amazing. Then suddenly Ali looked down and pointed:

"You!"

I looked around. His eyes were fixed on me and me alone. I stuck a finger in my chest:

"Me?"

"Yeah you chump, aren't you the one that called me a nigga?"

"No champ, I said you were BIGGER, bigger than life!"

My heart was thumping but I'd always been quick with the mouth and this got a rise out of the small crowd.

"Get up here chump!"

I climbed into the ring. We just shadowboxed for some thirty seconds with Ali clowning and showboating, but I was nervous. It was less being in the presence of this sports legend – the kind of jitters you might naturally have in meeting a famous head of state or international movie star – than the potential for utter destruction which loomed before me. It was just good fun, there was absolutely no chance that Ali would have actually thrown a punch at me, but it was all there just waiting to erupt at the flick of a switch. And you felt it. And of course he wanted you to feel it. Very humbling. I found out later they were filming a boxing documentary called *Down for the Count* and all this was caught on tape. But with the exception of a close-up of me on the ring apron staring up at the champ, our sparring session was edited out for the final TV version - though I was able to get a couple still shots of me standing next to Ali from one of the photographers at the event.

On some Saturdays I picked LC up and we drove twenty-five miles to the Goosen brothers' makeshift gym in North Hollywood. I remember the brothers' having houses on either side of a cul-de-sac and me changing into workout gear at one house then walking to the other where the backyard had a ring and some bags. At the "changing house" was a big tree stump that fighters could take an axe to for some old-school training. It was at the Goosens' place where I first sparred with a professional boxer, Walter Sims, a tough lightweight who had already had some dozen bouts. When you square off with your first experienced pro fighter, you quickly realize that you have a lot to learn! Sims definitely hit me more times than he missed. But I stayed three rounds and gave some back. Although he was just working with me, I got tired of being pounded and used my size advantage to push him into the ropes – not to be dirty but to give my body a reprieve from all the punishment! In the gym that day watching the action was Sonny Shields, father of welterweight fighter Randy Shields who went twelve rounds with Tommy "Hitman" Hearns in 1981. Sonny was a stuntman, a friend of my father in fact, and tremendously fit and tough. He looked like he could jump in the ring and spar ten rounds easy! In between rounds he gave me encouraging words: "Hang in there kid, keep punching."

I had little choice.

After three rounds with Walter Sims, LC worked the focus mitts with me, followed by five rounds on the heavy bag, a few on the speed bag, jumping rope, then ending the session with some stomach work. By the time I had finished, my head was pounding, a combination of taking hard blows to the noggin and dehydration. LC Morgan was pleased and told me on the drive back that he always dropped fighters who folded the first time sparring with a pro.

On the work front I was given responsibility for all custom products pertaining to the second-generation Stinger missile (FIM92-B) which was the weapon the U.S. supplied Afghan rebels with during the Soviet occupation of Afghanistan. At the time this program was headed by General Dynamics and was a shoulder-fired missile and offshoot of the original Redeye missile developed in the late 1960s. The Stinger along with a classified TRW space-related program were my top responsibilities. Both highly challenging from the chip-level standpoint. Since both were high-pressure and high-profile programs, I almost *needed* the boxing ring every evening to relieve my stress.

It was around this time that my father began performing in Las Vegas at the Dunes Hotel. I would take the short flight from Los Angeles to see his show. My father was raking in about ten-thousand dollars a week from the Dunes but making ten times that conning people out of their money backstage with his phantom movie deals. Being hip to his game, I observed Jimmy Lucas and Bob Mayo signaling each other as to which guests arriving for the show would be "marks" that night. What a waste of talent, I thought. At show's end, after my father had belted out his encore performance of "Vesti la Giubba" from the opera *Pagliacci*, I would go backstage and hear him talking crazy about movies and other pie-in-the-sky deals. A couple times he asked me to come work for him, which I just ignored. Maybe he was offended. Because it was shortly after his stint at the Dunes that he appeared on the Merv Griffin Show – a fact which I learned not from my father but my cousin Jerry. I grabbed a *TV Guide* and saw "Mario Casini" in the listing. That night my roommates and I gathered around the television to watch my father give a great performance of two Mario Lanza classics. This would definitely bolster his legitimacy as a vocal artist and give his career a real chance – if he only cut out the con artistry.

In the meantime the Joe Louis Memorial Gym had closed down, but LC told me about another great place to train – Broadway Gym in south-central Los Angeles on the corner of 108th Street and Broadway, and operated by Bill Slayton, who had briefly trained heavyweight champion Ken Norton. Due to distance and my schedule it was impossible for LC to continue training me, but what I now lacked in terms of LC's old-school style was made up for by the Broadway Gym's old-school atmosphere. Before you entered you could hear the sound of bags being pounded, the slap of jump ropes and trainers encouraging their fighters, and as soon as you walked in the smell was a mixture of sweat and wintergreen and raw menace.

Broadway is in a tough neighborhood, too, and from Playa Del Rey it took me about twenty minutes to drive there on surface streets. It was directly across the street from what appeared to be the clubhouse of a predominantly black motorcycle club called "The Chosen Few." During the course of your workout you consistently heard police and ambulance sirens going by. Although it was a dicey neighborhood, no one bothered me or any of the other fighters going in or out of the gym. At first, as one of the few white guys training at Broadway, I was a bit worried about not only my presence in a black neighborhood but parking my new Camaro out on the street, but nothing ever happened.

I ended up finding a good trainer there named Rudy Kinney who had also migrated from Joe Louis Memorial. Rudy already had a stable of fighters including an up and coming kid named Jimmy Nakahara. At Broadway Gym we were known as the night shift because we arrived at the gym at 6 pm and left just before it closed at 9 pm. There were two very active rings at Broadway, and many pros worked out there, so it was easy getting ring work. One of the pros I worked with a lot was Alphonso "The Bumblebee" Long. Super nice guy and a skillful and elusive fighter. (In 1989, Long fought Simon Brown for the IBF World Welterweight

Title but lost.) It was difficult to land a solid blow on Brown because of his speed and agility. Sometimes during our sparring sessions he would crouch so low that he disappeared completely from sight! Once I even turned completely around because I thought he'd gone behind me – only to feel a tap on the back of my head letting me know he'd been in front of me all along.

My first fight in California was held at the Compton YMCA on the corner of Rosecrans and Alameda. Another rough area. I entered the ring confident and in good shape weighing in at 156 lbs. Unfortunately, I was unable to contain my nervous energy. The first round was a disaster due to being overly aggressive. I found myself off balance and got tagged a couple times. I was never hurt, I mean this guy couldn't hurt me with a baseball bat, but the ref gave me a standing eight-count, which simply made me angry. It is never good to fight angry, but by the second round I had finally regained my composure. In round three I came on strong with controlled intensity, which I should have done from the outset. My opponent, who was my exact height and weight, began to noticeably fade after I caught him square in the nose. The blood was trickling over his lips and I could see in his eyes that he was just trying to survive the round. So I continued to move him back and make him fight on his heels. At this stage it was easy to walk through his punches. Then I delivered a savage uppercut to his body just the right side of his chest and causing him to buckle over. The ref stepped in presumably to give my opponent an eight-count. Instead he stood there and repeatedly asked if he was all right. I'm standing there waiting, knowing a couple more shots and he's done. The crowd begins to boo as between ten to fifteen seconds pass with no explanation. I wasn't reprimanded for a low blow, my punch was clearly legal, so I was as stunned as the crowd when the ref made no ruling at all. He just gave my opponent time to recover. Time was running out for me to close the deal and my corner was yelling at the ref as well. By the time action recommenced, I had only a few seconds to knock this kid out as he stood in the corner with his hands up and elbows in tight to fend off another body blow. The bell rang and it was over. He survived and squeaked out a victory as the crowd booed heavily then began throwing coins into the ring. This was a common gesture in those days, the crowd acknowledging your effort and in particular if they believed you had been the victim of a bad decision. My trainer told me the money was for me, but it's hard to pick up quarters and half-dollars with twelve-ounce gloves on, so I told my stablemates ringside they could have it. Even though I felt I won the fight, I also felt I *deserved* to lose for not being composed in the first round and part of the second. Lesson learned!

At work I was given added responsibility, specifically a high-profile TRW space program that entailed a half-million dollar early delivery. This was going to be a major challenge. There was no slack in the schedule for anything to go wrong. The pressure was on and I embraced it. To help insure early delivery, TRW provided me an in-house technical rep to make critical decisions on the spot. He was a mild-mannered gentleman in his late forties. The qualification process for these advanced custom space devices was about twenty-four weeks. The plan at TRW was to work round the clock so the critical device we were building could be plugged in at the last moment – and with us finishing in time to earn the bonus. Looking at the calendar, I saw the delivery deadline bumped up against the California Golden Gloves tournament. It was going to be arduous putting in the requisite training for it while also putting in the necessary overtime for the TRW program.

The TRW program went fairly smoothly – but it was not without some heated arguments with fellow employees. However nothing was ever taken personally because it was the nature of the job and part of a highly aggressive corporate culture; besides, everyone knew about the project and the tight timetable. I could tell that the consistent confrontation made the gentlemanly TRW representative uncomfortable, but the half-million dollar incentive was at risk as the deadline approached. We had shipped the flight units early and they were already installed in TRW's system awaiting the results of the advanced testing performed on a sample basis. I received this data the evening before the deadline and had to fax the results to the TRW division in Colorado before midnight in order for them to qualify for the early incentive. The fax went out just before 10 pm so we made it by a couple hours. Now I could focus on fighting, as the Golden Gloves prelim bouts were less than a week away.

I was excited to be fighting before a big crowd at the famed Olympic Auditorium. Not only had the Olympic hosted the boxing at the 1932 L.A. Olympics but numerous championship fights had taken place here. I won my preliminary bout fairly easily and advanced to the quarter-final. High school and college pals Kevin McAleer and Bart Devaney along with Bart's father attended this next bout and they were probably the only ones in the audience who knew that my real name was not "Castillo" – which is how the announcer at the Olympic pronounced my name. This wasn't the first time that had happened. For some reason they would see the name Costello and immediately assume I was Mexican. I didn't mind it this time, though, because the crowd at the Olympic was itself predominantly Mexican and cheered loudly upon hearing one of their own being announced – and particularly since I was fighting a black guy.

I came out very relaxed and worked my jab effectively, staying to the outside until I could assess the skill, speed and power of my opponent. After about a minute I double-jabbed and stepped in with a straight right but missed all three punches as my opponent was forced into the ropes by my momentum. He covered up right away instead of countering, which gave me the impression he was unwilling to go toe to toe. This encouraged me to increase the pressure and start cutting off the ring. The first round was fairly boring, mostly due to my opponent's unwillingness to engage. Because I had barely broken a sweat in the first round, I stepped it up in the second, beginning to cut off the ring more aggressively and throw more punches. I landed some effective shots while taking few in return. After the second round my trainer told me to cruise the third because he believed I would easily advance to the semi-final. But since I was in excellent boxing shape I wasn't inclined to take it easy. Besides, I had friends at ringside whom I wanted to impress.

Seems my opponent may have been holding back a bit himself, as he came out hard and backed me up and caught me in the eye with a straight right. It didn't faze me much apart from the surprise element so I kept my cool and methodically took him apart, snapping his head back on multiple occasions and resulting in a standing eight-count. After the count I immediately went downstairs to the body since my opponent had moved his hands way up to protect his head. Both corners simultaneously yelled thirty seconds so I knew I had some time to win by TKO. I threw a double hook, first to the body then to the head. The hook to the body connected well, but the hook to the head was less effective since my opponent was already moving away from the punch. It felt like another shot might put him on the mat – but as I pivoted off my back foot and threw a hard right, my opponent dropped his head and my fist caught him on the top of his skull. Now every fighter knows that a guy's skull is far harder than your knuckles, and twelve-ounce gloves plus hand wraps aren't always enough padding to protect your hand in this situation. I felt a sting go up my arm and past my elbow, then I felt my right glove get very tight. I was able to hide the injury by throwing stiff left jabs until the bell rang. It was clear I had won the fight. When they announced the winner as Juan Castillo, the ref grabbed my right glove and raised it in the air making me wince. My wince grew even bigger when it turned out my hand was so badly hurt that I'd be unable to fight in the semi-finals.

The next day after work I drove to the LMU campus to have the athletic trainer assess the damage. He could see it was in bad shape and referred me to the Kerlan-Jobe Clinic in Inglewood. These were guys who worked on professional athletes and had a reputation for excellence. The X-rays confirmed damage to the metacarpals just behind the knuckles of my index and middle fingers. I was given a lightweight fiber cast and sent home.

Returning to work the next day I found sitting on my desk the copy of a letter from TRW addressed to my CEO in which they thanked me for a job well done and confirmed that they had received the 500K incentive bonus for early delivery. This prompted me to call the TRW representative to thank him in turn and see how he was doing. The secretary who picked up the phone then informed me that the gentlemen had suffered a nervous breakdown shortly after he'd finished his duties as in-house rep.

On that same day we had representatives from AT&T in town to review the Towed Array Program – essentially a cable hung from the back of a ship and fitted with advanced sensors to pick up enemy submarines. These New Jersey guys were aware of my having fought two days earlier and I knew they would break my balls when they saw the cast on my hand, the noticeable mouse under my eye, and red glove burns on my cheek. As we sat down in the conference room they immediately started in:

"Johnny, what happened to your face?"

"Nothing – I was born like this."

"What about your hand?"

"I missed a payment to my New Jersey bookie."

"And you say you *won* the fight?"

"You should see the other guy!"

I had adjusted quickly to the white-collar world and felt confident in the boardroom doing presentations for executives both at my own firm and the companies of our customers. However, after working at my firm for a couple years I began to burn out and was looking for a change. I began to miss my cousins in Chicago and was planning a short trip there – a trip which led me to making one of the biggest mistakes of my life.

Ten

Risky Business

Periodically I would speak with my father, but not often. Usually before or just after watching him perform, which I actually enjoyed. I grew up listening to this type of music and had developed a taste for it. Each time we spoke he'd pitch me that he was 100 percent legit, showing me copies of the lucrative singing contracts he'd signed and asking me to move back to Chicago for a while and manage his career.

When I finally made it out to Chicago (to see my cousins) my father was performing at a southside Chicago club called the Sabre Room, which had a long history of artists like Frank Sinatra, Dean Martin, Tony Bennett, Bob Hope, Bill Cosby, B. B. King and George Burns. An old-school comedian named Jackie Gayle was the opening act at the Sabre Room this evening, followed by the female singer, then my father did his performance, and backstage after the show I saw him speaking with a young attractive girl about eighteen years old. I couldn't put my finger on it but there was something familiar about her. My father introduced her to me as Lori, and she and I hit it off fairly well. For the rest of the evening my father was on his best behavior and took the time to introduce me to some of the people milling around backstage. Some were involved with the show, others just guests of my father and, unbeknownst to me at the time, a couple of them major figures from the Chicago Outfit.

After the Sabre Room gig my father called me nonstop with news of all the other places he was going to perform. He even sent me the reviews from his shows in Vegas, swearing up and down that if I didn't manage him then others would jump at the opportunity. Although my career was on track and I enjoyed my friends in Los Angeles, I missed not only my cousins but the whole Chicago atmosphere. I finally and foolishly relented – though not before informing my company that I intended to return in a year or less and with them assuring me that I could step back into my job when I was again in California.

It was during those first couple days back in Chicago that I learned just why Lori and I got along so well and why she felt almost like a sister to me – because she *was* almost my sister. That is to say, my half-sister, the product of a liaison my father had had with Lori's mother Helen. Lori explained that Helen had been unaware of my father's marital status at the time and that it had been a fleeting indiscretion, namely a one-night stand and Lori the result. I listened closely and offered no comment. Roughly a week later I was looking at some old black-and-white pictures hanging in the basement of my crazy paternal grandmother. When I came across a picture of my mother and inquired about the woman she was within the photo, my grandmother was hesitant. I pressed for an answer and she capitulated by telling me the woman's name was Helen, a friend of my mother. Then I asked if Helen had a daughter named Lori. Now my grandmother was very uncomfortable, but thinking I'd be upset if I didn't get an answer, she responded in the affirmative. Not that this placated me. Even worse was when I found out that Helen was married at the time of the affair. Yes, an affair, not some drunken one-night stand, and just as I had suspected. Suspicions confirmed to me by my paternal aunts. To this day I don't know all the details, but Lori was certainly covering for her mother's less-than-enviable behavior; or else her mother had sold her on the story. I mean, I don't want to sound moralistic or anything, but a double-adultery with the husband of your ostensible friend can make even the worst of us feel a bit tainted. As for my father, I wasn't surprised. I'd already been through all this years before with his replacement family.

My old high-school friend Juan Azcarate had driven with me from Los Angeles to Chicago and was staying for a week or so. Not that he'd picked the best time of year. December in the windy city can be bone-chillingly cold. We'd been in Chicago several days when my father invited us both to dinner at The Viking Restaurant, an upscale place just outside of town. We got into our overcoats and drove to a place several miles from the restaurant where I parked my car and then Juan and I climbed into my father's new Caddy. He had a large wad of bills he flashed and which told me he'd made a score and was playing the big shot that evening. At the restaurant we had a nice meal and afterward went to the lounge – where who should be waiting for us but Lori, her mother Helen, and Lori's boyfriend Tom. (I found out later that they had been seated at a table in another part of the restaurant, my father picking up their check.) Right away I didn't like the look of things. Tom impressed me as an arrogant jerk. Helen was drunk and being embarrassingly flirty with my father. Meantime I was observing Lori who seemed to share my distaste for her mother's suggestive behavior. Or she was simply disturbed that I was personally witnessing it – after all, theirs had only been a "one-night stand."

I conversed with Juan, trying to ignore Helen, but my distaste was rapidly turning to disgust. Eventually Juan and

I drifted from the table to confer privately about what was going on – he was just as bothered by this train wreck as I was – and getting the hell out of there. Helen and Tom left the table too, leaving Lori to speak with my/her father. From across the lounge I could tell that Lori and he were arguing. Fifteen minutes later Helen and Tom returned to the table. Juan and I then walked back to the table to retrieve my father's keys in order to pick up my car; twenty minutes later we returned with the keys and as I approached the table again I could sense the tension between Tom and my father. I sat on the edge of the booth with Tom to the left of me.

My father's eyes were shooting daggers at Tom – who wasn't cowed and appeared equally pissed off. That entire time in the lounge all I'd been able to think about was the betrayal of my mother at the hands of Helen and my father, and now all I could hear in my head were the last words I had spoken to my mother. That I hated her. My heart began to race and my head to pound. I was overflowing with adrenalin that needed a release. My father kept muttering that he was about to "do something."

"Is there a problem?" I asked tight-lipped.

Tom gave me a disdainful look: "You can mind your own . . ."

BAM!

It was probably the hardest I've ever hit someone inside or outside the ring. Behind that punch was the weight of 24 years of anger and resentment. Though it wasn't on the chin, so he didn't go down. But I could feel his orbital bone collapse. Then I followed up with a hook and a right cross, both landing on the top of his head as he lunged and tackled me onto the table next to ours and sending the glasses of wine flying. We slid off the table onto the floor and he was on top of me trying to grab my neck but with his face down in my chest, presumably so as not to be struck again. With my left hand I grabbed his hair to pull his head up and briefly saw the gash above his eye as he once more turtle-shelled on my chest, gripping my suit and burying his face while I continued punching him on both sides of his head. Some restaurant employees jumped in to bust things up. As they grabbed us one of them accidentally stepped on my right hand in the same spot where I had broken it in the Golden Gloves.

There were two guys on either side of me telling me to "calm down." I assured them I was cool as could be – as I looked around for Tom. I was intent on inflicting more damage. Helen and Lori were screaming at my old man. I could feel an abrasion on my neck but remember being more concerned about all the blood on my nice dress shirt. Juan and I started to leave the restaurant, but before we made the exit there stood Tom. I said:

"I'm going to bury you, punk."

"Fuck you asshole."

"Talking pretty brave for a guy that just got his face rearranged."

"Eat shit."

"You should have asked my sister to fight me."

Schoolyard stuff. But I was steaming. I walked toward him but there were too many people between us for me to reach him again.

Juan and I headed out the door just as two sheriff's deputies were coming into the restaurant. I covered my blood-stained shirt with the flap of my overcoat and said: "It's a madhouse in there." They continued past and when Juan and I made the sidewalk my father was waiting for us at the curb in his Caddy. He had a smile on his face. Had he set the whole thing up? Knowing I would react like Pavlov's dog if Tom mouthed off to me? Was I reading too much into that smile? But whether he had played me again or not – it didn't matter. In a weird way I felt that I had honored my mother's memory by exacting some retribution against Helen albeit through her daughter's boyfriend. I'm not saying I'm proud of the episode, but none of us had behaved with any kind of regal tact. Not even Lori – who may have been misled herself but who in my mind had blatantly lied to me about Helen and my father.

In fact the only person without reproach was Juan. I was also impressed by how calm he remained – considering he was unaccustomed to this type of violence close up.

It was after Juan left that I settled into an apartment just outside the city. One day I drove out to Downers Grove to meet with my father and a couple of his friends at a place called The Pointe. These were two of the guys I had seen backstage after one of his shows. I was reintroduced to Marco D'Amico and Salvatore "Solly" Delaurentis, both handsome men in finely tailored suits. And with an intimidating aura about them. Marco's mannerisms were very polished – his posture, the way he smoked his cigarette and held his drink all denoted a certain elegance. Solly D was more your meat-and-potatoes guy. After the pleasantries the ball-breaking commenced.

"What's wrong wid your kid?" Solly said to my father. "Nice college boy turning the Viking lounge into a laundromat!"

"Yeah Mario," echoed Marco. "What kind of a hoodlum are you raising – starting all that trouble in a public place?"

I sat there a bit nervous and uncertain how to react. It seemed all in good fun, but the last thing I wanted to do was say something to piss these guys off. To be on the safe side I smiled, nodded my head in agreement and repeated a line I'd heard a thousand times from other Italian kids in my neighborhood:

"You know, you're right – and when you're right you're right."

They laughed, not expecting this typical tough-guy response from an LA college boy. Then they started talking about my father's next show – at the Carlisle Room in suburban Oak Brook. The Carlisle! Among other things it was known for high-profile mob weddings . . .

I was glad I'd told them they were right.

My father had opened an office just outside of Chicago and it was there we started planning the Carlisle show and others that followed. One of my duties was to secure the talent, namely the opening comedian followed by a female performer. I was also selling tables for the event at a grand each. My father had certain tables in the front of the showroom reserved for VIPs which included high-level members of the Chicago Outfit as well as famed local business guys like Nick Cellozzi, owner of Celozzi-Ettleson Chevrolet which at one time was the largest Chevy dealer in the country. A number of politicians and members of law enforcement were also typically given reserved seating at these shows. This of course made for some awkward moments, especially when I had to give advance instructions to the hired photographer as to what tables to avoid when taking pictures. Although the guest-list for these events gave me pause, all seemed to be on the up and up – until a few months later, that is, when I was instructed to pick up money in unorthodox ways.

Go meet Chris on such and such street, his limo will be parked and he is expecting you at 9:00 pm – don't be late!

I'd meet with him multiple times and bring back at least 25K in an envelope. I found out later that "Chris" was a Chicago bookmaker. On another occasion I was told to go to Heritage Bank out in Blue Island and meet up with so and so.

He'll look for your car in the parking lot and hand you a briefcase – don't be late!

Then I started to notice who was coming in and out of the office. I became accustomed to interfacing with these men and found them intriguing. I must admit that this cloak-and-dagger lifestyle had a certain appeal compared to the mundane white-collar world I had just left. Many of these Outfit guys were treated like celebrities, and when I was with them I was treated in the same fashion. It was addictive and I'd be lying if I claimed I didn't enjoy it. But still I was reticent about taking any salary from my father's company (Fortune Productions) outside of direct expenses. I mostly lived off the money I had made at my previous job along with a percentage of the revenue generated from the shows.

But my father knew I was accustomed to earning a steady paycheck, and in an effort to "sweeten the pot" he had sent me to see Cook County Sheriff Richard J. Elrod.

This needs a word of explanation.

Elrod had a long history in Chicago politics and law enforcement and was something of a living legend. It seems my father's relationship with him dated back to my paternal grandfather. While doing well in real estate, my grandfather was dragged into the rough and tumble world of Chicago politics by his son, who somehow had a stake in the election bid of a certain Jerome Feldman for Alderman of the 50th Ward. My grandfather gave financial backing to Feldman, who ultimately lost, but through whatever machinations both my father and grandfather then became involved with Richard Elrod. This was back in the 1960s, so Elrod and my old man went back a long ways. Their relationship was a mysterious one, but it was apparent Elrod owed my father a favor since I was now going for a personal audience with this powerful individual.

When I walked into his office he didn't stand up to shake hands. This didn't surprise me. It was well-known that Elrod was partially paralyzed from the shoulders down, the result of a broken neck incurred in 1969 during a demonstration led by the "Weathermen" faction of Students for a Democratic Society. I joined him sitting and he engaged me in small talk about my college and work experience. When he spoke of my father an enigmatic smile crept across his face – which seemed to communicate that he knew Mario to be quite the character.

"So your father says you're looking for part-time work," said Elrod. "How would you like to be made a Deputy Sheriff?"

I'd heard tell that it was common practice for the Cook County Sheriff to offer patronage jobs as part-time Deputy Sheriffs to friends and political backers. I'd also heard that not only were most of these appointees seriously unqualified to wear a badge – let alone carry a gun – but that quite a number of them were convicted felons. This didn't stop me from saying:

"I don't really have the training for that kind of thing. I mean, don't you need police-academy credentials or something?"

Again that enigmatic smile – this time saying: *You're not exactly like your father, are you?*

We spoke a bit more, he making it clear that the job was mine if I wanted, training or no training, and I ended by respectfully telling him that I'd need time to think about it. Of course I never took up his offer, but that's not to say that this politically unconnected 24-year-old kid didn't go away from that talk duly impressed – when it came to deputizing people, Wyatt Earp had nothing on Sheriff Elrod![3]

---

3 The most infamous example of this fast and loose style of deputization is the well documented case of the mob hitmen who failed to kill Ken Eto, an alleged mob bookie who became a liability after being arrested. The

And the Sultan of Brunei had nothing on my father.

At that time he was spending lavishly and found myriad ways of blowing money instead of investing in the marketing of his talent and in consistently performing so as to build a fan-base for his music. This was a source of great frustration to me. Most knew of the friction between me and my father – in large part because I openly argued with him in the office when others were present, including guys like Ronnie Ross, Eddie Caruso and Johnny Unger. You see, I knew exactly how much money my father was taking out of the company, my father's Outfit friends did not. Using money from the company he would put a down payment on an expensive house, buy cars and run up bills at high-priced restaurants. Then came the topper when he decided to buy his own Italian restaurant. We fought vehemently over this colossal splurge. Like everything else he bought, he would make the down payment and then ride it out as long as he could without paying – or by paying the absolute minimum – so as to keep the restaurant's doors open. Now he was in a position to run up his credit-line from suppliers of the restaurant. My father asked long-time friend and restaurateur Johnny Abbatacola to manage the restaurant renamed "Mario's Place." It was probably no accident that Johnny was the brother-in-law of tenor Mario Lanza, the singer my father had emulated in his youth.

Although I had been against the restaurant purchase, I would hang out there and fall into conversation with some of

---

hitmen shot Eto three times in the head, but Eto miraculously survived and became a government witness – which is what the mob had been trying to prevent in the first place by ordering his murder. So now the failed hitmen had to go, and the decomposing bodies of Jasper Campise and John Gattuso were later found in the trunk of a car. As I recall, either one or both had Deputy Sheriff badges on them when they were discovered. It was amidst all the controversy surrounding part-time deputies and other federal investigations that Sheriff Elrod lost the 1986 election (to his Undersheriff James O'Grady)but then went on to be appointed by the Illinois Supreme Court as a Cook County Circuit Judge.

my father's mob friends and associates. Drinking with these guys and listening to their stories was fascinating. Before airing their secrets they would start by saying that they had spoken to someone who vouched for me – which was a nod to my trustworthiness but also a veiled warning. *This goes no further than this table.* One night I was sitting at the bar with Ronnie Ross and having a single-malt scotch when two older guys sat down next to me. One identified himself as Dominic Volpe – part of the "over-the-hill gang" he added smilingly. He introduced the other guy to me as his "driver," who just bobbed his head in acknowledgement. Dominic said he wanted to show me something and said I could bring my friend Ronnie. The two of us got in my car and we followed Dominic and his driver to a place called The Round Up, a shit-kicking country-western place. What the fuck? We all got out and went to the front entrance where the bouncers stood.

Bouncer: "Howdy Mr. Volpe!"

Dominic: "How are youse guys?"

Bouncer: "We're just fine, thankee."

Dominic: "Dese cowpokes are wid me."

They waved us through. Now I'm really confused. The joint is packed with people in Western duds and we're walking through the heart of the club dressed in suits and catching inquisitive looks from all the make-believe wranglers. We get to the kitchen and go down a small staircase leading to a basement. The first thing I notice while walking down is a classic car – might have been an old Mustang – at the bottom of the staircase and roped off like some type of display. To our left is the kind of bar you'd see in a high-end hotel – tranquil, classy, dimly lit and stocked with top-shelf liquor. Just when I thought I'd have to break out my lasso and start punching dogies. A far cry from the country-western stuff upstairs. A Sinatra song played softly as a bow-tied bartender asked me what I wished to drink. I kept with the scotch as Ronnie walked over to take a closer look at the car. Dominic turned to me:

"Kid, in the old days this is the place all the crews used to come to whack up all the dough they collected during the week."

I must have mumbled something in reply. I was looking around. Along with the bar the rest of the place was nicely appointed and spacious, and we were the only ones in it, not even any decorative floozies.

"You come here any time you want, kid. No tabs, no tipping. You order whatever you want from the kitchen and they'll whip it up."

His driver was sitting at the bar with us but hadn't uttered a word since having been first introduced. Mob guys probably liked that – a guy who wouldn't talk. Or maybe they'd ripped out his tongue as a precautionary measure. Dominic stuck a finger in my face.

"The invitation is for *you* only." Then he gestured at Ronnie: "He ain't allowed in here after tonight."

I nodded.

"You wanna bring a little guma" – short for *gumare* which was Italian street slang for girlfriend – "you're welcome to dat too."

We ordered some sausage and peppers from the kitchen and then called it a night. Walking back through all the cowfolk on the upper level I felt like cutting loose with *Whoopee-ti-yi-yo!* This underworld lifestyle was becoming more and more seductive.

Then several events caused our situation to unravel. Chris, the guy I would periodically meet in his limo to pick up money, was arrested in a major drug bust by the Chicago Police Department's Organized Crime Division. Then there was Anthony and Michael Spilotro. I had met them on a couple occasions, once in Las Vegas and another time at his restaurant called Hoagies in Chicago. Everyone knew there were some serious issues going on in Vegas, so when Tony and Michael Spilotro failed to show for a scheduled court appearance the rumors were rampant. Most presumed they were dead but would never be found. However an Indiana farmer plowing his cornfield came across the murdered brothers' shallow grave. When someone goes to the trouble of burying two corpses at a farm in Indiana, you know these bodies were never meant to be uncovered. Someone was in trouble and repercussions were sure to follow.

Things at the office began to blow up as well. Reporters had been tipped off by someone, likely a disgruntled investor, and were starting their own investigation of Fortune Productions. A couple articles in the Chicago papers began questioning the legitimacy of my father's projects, thus alerting the authorities and worse yet my father's friends in the Chicago Outfit. This came to a head when the well-known Chicago TV reporter John Drummond did an investigative piece that aired on the local news three times in one night. The report included statements by the Chicago DA and a witness who was shown being interviewed incognito so as not to reveal his identity. This was about to get ugly, as my father's associates began asking questions and these guys always settled out of court, as it were. This led to the sit-down where I was cleared of any wrongdoing and – though it might sound like a bad play on words – I got a reputation for being a "stand-up" guy. My father walked away as well but was lucky to only have his credibility destroyed and not his life or any limbs. He split to Florida and resumed another operation because his antics would no longer be tolerated in Chicago. As I've already said, I'm convinced that had the mob not been so enamored of my father's singing talent and so captive to his charm, he would surely have been made an example of. And strange as it may seem, I remained in good graces with many of those associated with the Chicago Outfit. So much so that Eddie Caruso offered me a job and invited me to go on his "route" to experience things first-hand.

This was similar to taking-your-son-to-work-day – only difference being that Eddie didn't put in a long hard day to earn his paycheck but just stopped in at various places to pick up cash. Nice work if you can get it. I tagged along to some fairly stressful meetings, sit-downs really, but with someone other than myself in the hot seat. Eddie was highly effective in his job. There was one meeting with a guy who was late in paying. We were in a secluded construction trailer as Eddie listened patiently to the guy explain why he was unable to cough up. He went on and on with a number of seemingly very valid reasons for his inability to fork over the requisite cash.

"I've been sick and have doctor bills, my car broke down and it cost a lot to fix, I'm being audited, business is slow . . ."

And Eddie's compassionate reply: "So where's the fuckin' money?"

I recalled having heard that line somewhere before.

Then one day I received a phone call from Pete Antico. Pete was an established stuntman who had once dated my older sister. He had attended one of my father's shows at the Carlisle Room and was aware of all the connections I had in Chicago. Now he needed help for a friend of his named Tim Mansur. Tim owned a small produce business and was allegedly being "shaken down" by a guy named Jack Catain. It seems that at the time Catain was involved with whiz kid Barry Minkow in some type of illegal activity – in any event he had a reputation and Mansur was looking for a way to get him off his back. Pete asked if I could lend some assistance. I explained the situation to Eddie Caruso and he gave me the go-ahead to check it out and get back to him. This presented a good opportunity to return to LA and visit some friends while I was in town. While there I also met up with Tim. He told me he was scared and described a couple incidents that had been designed to intimidate him. I listened intently and told him I would get back to him after I reviewed the situation with my Chicago cohorts.

I flew back to Chicago that night. In returning to my apartment I ran into my neighbor. He mentioned that while I'd been gone there had been a number of people who'd come to my door. He said they looked like plainclothes cops. I entered my apartment and immediately checked my message machine. The first message was from the Federal Marshal asking to meet with me to discuss Fortune Productions. The second message was a cryptic death threat that shook me up but not so much as one might think. (Death threats are like threatened suicides – people who make prior announcements usually don't carry them out.) The third call was from Tim Mansur.

"Hey John, it's Tim. I forgot to tell you something. Call me when you get this message."

That was it. No stress or urgency in his voice, so I figured I'd call him in the morning.

Then the fourth message – from Pete Antico:

"John, Tim's dead."

Pete's voice went on to say that he'd died in the back of a Simi Valley Police car while being transported to the hospital. The police and others claimed drugs were involved, but Pete insisted that Tim had never been into drugs.

It was very late but I called Eddie anyway. I told him all that had transpired in LA as well as the phone messages.

Eddie coolly explained that "some things" were going down in both Chicago and Vegas, so I should lay low for a while. That night I slept sitting up with my back to the wall and a 44-caliber revolver in hand. I put a chair in front of me and hung my arms over its back so as to remain propped up and ready to drill anyone coming through my door or window. I was paranoid. But the pressure I felt wasn't imagined, it was real, the combined weight of recent events which had finally taken their toll.

Over the next couple weeks the Fortune Productions office was closed, as was the restaurant, and law enforcement was breathing down my neck. After days of avoiding calls from the authorities, I picked up the phone. They requested a meeting with me at my apartment. I preferred a public place because I wasn't persuaded they were law enforcement to begin with, and I made this clear to the guy on the phone who had identified himself simply as an "agent." I scheduled something over a week out. I had no intention of meeting with them. Not only was I unconvinced that I was dealing with true law enforcement but I knew that *if* they turned out to be the real thing then taking a meeting with them would not go over well with the Outfit guys. A lose-lose scenario. Then I read in the *Chicago Tribune* about the murder of a guy whom I had once met. Shot to death in a bingo parlor of all places. This wasn't glamour but sordid shit. Four acquaintances murdered in as many months. A day later I called Eddie and thanked him for the job offer but told him I was going back to California. This was no life for me.

At the Carlisle Room outside of Chicago with Eddie Caruso, my half-sister, college pals Vince Pangrazio, Frank Kennedy and Hollywood stuntman Pete Antico.

My paternal grandparents.

My mother and maternal grandparents standing in front of their north Chicago two-flat.

My newlywed parents.

*Headed to California
circa 1969.*

Little League Baseball

*Pop Warner Football
in 1972.*

My hard-ass father circa 1979.

At Crespi High School, sports became my sanctuary from the "imposter" family.

Back to the streets of Chicago with cousins from left to right "Iron" Mike Ecklund and Tony "Big Tones" Pacino aka Andrzejczak.. In the background is neighborhood pal Dave Sargis who later died of a cocaine overdose. Tony went on to become a Homicide Detective. Decades later Iron Mike would violently take his own life.

*The Loyola Marymount University varsity crew about to race at
the Newport Regatta, which we went on to win.*

*My chance meeting with Muhammad Ali at the
Joe Louis Memorial Gym in 1984.*

My father backstage at the Dunes Casino in Las Vegas with Milton Berle, who warmed up a sold-out audience on opening night.

My father admiring his name on the Dunes marquis.

Just after my first "official" fight in California at the YMCA in Compton.

Some college pals including teammates from the BSA 83 intramural football team.

My surprise birthday party was the first time my worlds collided.

What appears to be a surveillance photo mailed to me with no return address in front of "Da Big Smoke" cigar lounge includes Carmine Esposito, Louis Ippolito, Sonny D'Angelo and yours truly.

At a party thrown in honor of my friend Rusty Coones, who played the character Quinn in the popular FX series "Sons of Anarchy" at the Hells Angels clubhouse.

My cousin Iron Mike shortly after being released from Milan Federal Prison.

My father, while on probation, unaware that Henry Hill is at his table. Hill was in witness protection at the time.

Celebrating both Johnny Fratto's and his son Johnny Jr.'s birthday at my house with his immediate family. Rudy Fratto and Rudy Jr. along with others attended including my godson David Ruiz, friends Terry "The Tramp" Orendorff and Dennis Grindeland.

My lovely wife Janell at a Halloween party.

Over the years I had several intriguing conversations with the late legendary Hollywood producer Aaron Spelling. A very nice man with a great sense of humor.

I have encountered actor Jon Voight at various events including Larry Elder's Hollywood Walk of Fame ceremony where this photo was taken.

My initial introduction to Fred Durst during Limp Bizkit's heyday was a bit awkward as I ignorantly asked him what he did for a living. After I acknowledged my embarrassment, Fred laughed then graciously invited me to his next concert as a VIP.

200 miles off the California coast with two naval officers on the USS John C. Stennis as a Distinguished Visitor. These young men and women serving their country are something to behold. I had the good fortune of being invited back again on the USS Carl Vinson shortly after the Osama bin Laden operation.

The baptism of my first set of twins. Godparents Margie Brockert and Scott Baio, middle, Jim and Sheila Peterson on the far right. Scott and Jimmy P - two stand-up guys!

My wife and eldest set of twins at a family event with good friend Jimmy Van Patten aka "Jimmy from Queens" and his classy father, the late Dick Van Patten.

Here I am surrounded by very smart men (from left to right) California Congressman and Chairman of the House Armed Services committee, Howard "Buck" McKeon, nationally syndicated talk show host, Larry Elder, and Florida Congressman Colonel Alan West in Santa Clarita, California.

Fishing off the coast of Mexico on the CEO's yacht with fellow corporate executives.

Celebrating New Years with screenwriter producer Michael Berk. Mike, best-known for Soul Surfer and Baywatch, was one of the first people in the entertainment field I befriended.

For several years Hef hosted an Easter-egg hunt and petting zoo for the kids at the Playboy Mansion.

144

My pal Scott Baio and I were honored to meet Vice Admiral Gerald Beaman (ret.). At the time VADM Beaman was commander of the U. S. 3rd Fleet near San Diego, California.

I had the opportunity of briefing Chairman of the Senate Armed Services Committee, Senator John McCain, along with several other corporate executives, on a critical national security issue.

Having a private word with Senator McCain at the town-hall he held in the lobby of our secure facility in Phoenix, Arizona.

After a brief conversation about ITAR (International Trade and Arms Regulation) with Vice Admiral Joseph Rixey, Director of the Defense Security Cooperation Agency, we took this picture in front of an F-18 Super Hornet at the Farnborough Airshow in the UK.

I met four-star General Stanley A. McChrystal at an industry event in Virginia. General McChrystal led the Joint Special Operations Command in Iraq during the Persian Gulf Wars and was top commander of American forces in Afghanistan.

In the cockpit of an MH-60 Black Hawk helicopter with aerospace industries executive and friend, the retired Army Colonel Paul Paolozzi and two other of America's finest.

Nabbed a selfie with Karl Rove, Senior Advisor and Deputy Chief of Staff for the George W. Bush administration at an event in Scottsdale, Arizona.

Eleven

After my Chicago experience I was relieved to return to Los Angeles and reunite with all my friends and work colleagues. However my ordeal was far from over because the Chicago DA was still building a case against me and my father. Me only because my name was on the corporate paperwork. The newspapers in both Chicago and Florida covered the story while making sure to mention all my father's aliases when describing his alleged crimes, then with the tag line "and his son" – thus implicating me as well. I wasn't terribly worried because for one thing there was no paper trail of money leading to me, and secondly all those people that my father took for money never interfaced with me. But just to be sure, I made an unannounced call to my father's attorney. The moment he picked up he told me not to tell him where I was because he (the attorney) might be under indictment as well. He went on to say there was already a 92-page indictment with my name included, but he also verified my hunch that the authorities weren't pursuing me. My father later ended up beating most of the charges in Chicago but in Florida was charged with nearly a dozen felonies including racketeering and grand theft. He kept his mouth shut and simply pleaded out on six of them while the others were dropped.

The big con man was now a con in the Florida prison system.

At first glance my entire Chicago experience might appear to be an epic fail. For a long time I thought as much myself. The risks I took were unacceptable for a person just starting his career. But I learned about human behavior in its rawest form. Anthropology 101, you might say, with the only difference being that "F" didn't mean flunking the course but *finito*. I learned how to apply stress overtly and covertly, measuring action and reaction at primal levels, and got a master class in exploiting a person's vulnerabilities. I felt that this experience would give me an edge in the corporate world by learning to handle situations that most white-collar guys would never experience or even relate to – but I will say that as the years went on I realized the corporate world was simply the Chicago Outfit minus the physical mayhem.

Within a week of returning to Los Angeles, I started back at the company I had left. One of my first objectives was to achieve some semblance of normalcy in my day-to-day life. Reestablishing my career was a good start but I needed something more so that I would never even consider drifting back to the underworld. I was moving up the corporate food chain, my finances were in decent shape, I had a good circle of friends, wasn't hanging with the wrong crowd, but the one thing missing was a certain female presence in my life. All these years I hadn't exactly been a monk, though the truth is I'd never had a serious girlfriend. I'm no psychiatrist but one thing I can tell you is that when you're carrying a ton of guilt and hate around in your heart, it's not difficult to become emotionally detached.

But enough was enough.

It was time to break out of this cold lonely prison I found myself in.

I began dating a woman named Tina – short for Valentina – whom I met through my friend Juan Azcarate. Tina was a petite brunette with a cute figure. Her green eyes were flecked with gold which gave them an uncanny glitter. She was in her family's manicuring business. She loved animals and rode horses competitively. She was kind and sensitive, had a good head on her shoulders, and seemed the right woman at the right time.

I was in my late twenties and looking to settle down. My finances were in order, as mentioned, but for marriage I still needed greater financial stability, so once a high-paying sales job became available at my company I jumped at it and snagged the position. It was refreshing to get out of the office to visit customers. The company had transferred its headquarters to Burbank so I decided to move from Playa del Rey to the San Fernando Valley with four other guys from work. The house was over 4000 square feet and it soon became party central. These were fun but I needed to offset that kind of thing with regular vigorous exercise. Unfortunately there were no boxing gyms close by that stayed open late enough for me to train. There was one in Van Nuys that I visited a couple times and worked with an accomplished heavyweight named John Bray. But my schedule wasn't conducive to the gym's operating hours so I put my boxing on hold for a while.

Anyway I was now focused on work and Tina. We dated for a year and the wedding took place in March 1988. My groomsmen were all college buddies and my Best Man was Kevin McAleer. Performing the marriage ceremony was Father John – the same Father John whose principal's office had been blitzkrieged by my father a decade earlier. Since he was incarcerated, Mr. and Mrs. McAleer were my stand-in parents. Though jokey about it, Mr. McAleer had been a bit concerned as to how this might go over with my jailbird father.

"When's his release date? When do I enter the Witness Protection Program?"

"Mr. Mac, you let me worry about my father."

All this carried more than a little symbolism. I knew Mr. McAleer as a good solid family man, the exact opposite of my father, and that was precisely my goal – to be a faithful, responsible and supportive husband. I was looking forward to fatherhood and to providing my kids with the love and caring that had eluded me, Billy and Margie.

Within a year of our being married, Tina was pregnant. But our excitement turned to sadness when an ectopic pregnancy was confirmed. Most ectopic pregnancies form in the Fallopian tube and can be physically painful. Not to mention the emotional pain. Tina suffered in both regards, and I tried my best to comfort her throughout the ordeal, which only reinforced my awareness of just how defenseless she could sometimes be. I'd always been protective of her, but after witnessing this vulnerability I resolved to be even more shielding in the future.

Soon after that I left the small private firm I'd been with and accepted a sales job at a larger public semiconductor company along with a nice bump in salary and benefits. With our financial situation improving, Tina and I decided to move from our small apartment in Northridge and buy a condo in a gated community in Newhall just a few miles outside of the San Fernando Valley. Then we tried again for a baby. During this process we had to carefully time things in order to maximize our chances. This sometimes entailed Tina leaving her work early and me as well. One of our afternoon rendezvous I arrived at our condo to find her very upset. She explained that on the way home she had stopped at a full-service gas station and asked the attendant to put ten dollars in the tank. She was short on cash and only had a twenty for gas and a quick stop at the supermarket to make some purchases for dinner. Seems the attendant put in twenty dollars worth and when Tina protested he snatched the twenty from her hand and made a derogatory remark. I asked her which service station and who the attendant was – some Middle Eastern guy named Mohammed. Tina freely gave me this information; though she'd heard stories of my violent side, in our marriage I'd kept a tight lid on it. I stayed calm throughout our talk, then the next morning I just as calmly adjusted my sales-call schedule in order to be in the neighborhood of the service station.

I wanted to make the acquaintance of this Mohammed.

I pulled up to the station near the phone booth, got out pretending to make a call but saved myself a quarter by just surveying the station to see if a Middle Easterner was working, which there was. And no apparent security cameras. They weren't that common back then but some places had them. I got back in my car and pulled up to the full-serve. The guy came out to gas my car – on his shirt said "Mohammed."

"Twenty dollars regular."

He put the gas in my Caddy then stuck the nozzle back on the pump.

"That will be twenty dollars."

"What? What the fuck's wrong with you jagoff! I clearly said *ten dollars* – take the fucking kabobs out of your ears."

"You said twenty!"

He's pointing at me. I walk toward him, my hand going to my pocket pretending to take out the money, and when I get close enough I grab his head with my right hand and slam it into the gas pump. It's less my action than its shock and surprise that causes him to trip over the pump's raised platform and hit the ground. He screams for his workmates. I stand over him and contemptuously peel off a ten. A tall black dude comes out of the mechanic bay and then another Middle Eastern guy, heavy-set, runs out of the office screaming at me:

"I call the police! I call the police!"

"Go ahead! This prick tried to rob me!"

I was moving toward the heavy-set guy when the mechanic held his hand out to prevent me from getting any closer. They helped Mohammed up and said they were calling the police as all three turned and walked off. I got back in my car and drove away.

Heading to my first sales call I went over the episode in my mind. They said they'd call the cops but I doubted it. And even if they did, there wasn't much to go on. No security cameras and they didn't seem to have noted my license-plate number. The only thing that bothered me was the thickset guy also had "Mohammed" on his shirt.

Shit, I hope I got the right Mohammed.

But returning home that evening I just told Tina I'd straightened out the asshole at the gas station.

"You did what?"

"I straightened him out – you know, taught him a lesson."

"What do you mean by that?"

"Nothing much – just slammed his head against the pump."

"You could have been arrested!"

"Oh, and I got our ten dollars back."

The upshot was that while she appreciated my standing up for her, she felt it a complete overreaction. Which it was. If you're coming at it from your average everyday perspective, that is. But my perspective had been skewed from the get-go. Although in a physical sense I was inhabiting the prosperous California suburbs, my mind was still roaming the Chicago streets, a world of casual violence and getting even. By Tina's standards my behavior was reprehensible and verging on psychopathic – by my own lights I was just doing the minimum necessary to keep my self-respect.

By the summer of 1993 we had conceived another child but the pregnancy was once again ectopic. Tina and I were both very down as she went through the painful process of surgery. This time her one remaining Fallopian tube had to be removed. The only option left was in-vitro fertilization – something I wasn't crazy about.

And there was more misfortune in store. I got a phone call from my younger brother Bill and his first words were: "Bad news – Gino's dead."

Killed in a motorcycle accident. On the spot. July 26th 1993. His twentieth birthday.

Gino was my half-brother and had been a baby when I first moved in with my father and his "imposter" family. But even though Gino was part of this incursion my resentment never included him specifically – not only because he himself wasn't responsible, but the fact is we got along really well. And became fairly close. In our last conversation he'd told me he wanted to leave Chicago. I said he was welcome to stay with me until he got on his feet. Gino was a handsome kid, a nice build, seal-brown eyes and with a pleasant and likeable disposition. I have no idea where he got this last part. Maybe some recessive Canadian gene.

I flew back to Chicago leaving Tina behind. I wasn't going to put her through a Costello wake and funeral – you never knew what might happen. The whole flight I thought about Gino. My most distinct memory was teaching him how to fight when he was ten or eleven years old. He was having problems with a bully at school so I told him exactly what to do – don't respond in kind to taunts or shoving matches but just pop him in the nose. Immediate escalation is very effective and in Gino's case it worked like a charm. One coachable kid. I remember him coming back elated from his initial application of the Costello method. He wasn't aggressive by any means, just proud and gutsy, and I had a long and depressing flight.

By this time my father had made parole and was living in Chicago. I had no desire to see him, we'd hardly communicated since our rift, but if anything could have occasioned a further meeting between us it was Gino's death. When I got to his place he was more shook up than I'd ever seen him. He looked older – but prison, the death of your son – I suppose that'll do it.

It was an awkward embrace.

"Johnny, I want you to be a pallbearer for Gino."

"Sure thing."

"He always liked you, always talked nice about you."

"He was a good kid."

We were quiet. My father had a glisten of tears in his eyes – or what I took to be a glisten of tears. I'd never seen tears from him before, so couldn't be sure.

"I need you to do me a favor, Yuma."

Here it comes I thought, more skullduggery, more double-dealing, on the eve of his own son's funeral . . .

"What's that?"

"Someone needs to go back to his apartment and sort through his things. I can't do it – his mother can't do it –"

"No problem."

But it was a problem. Don't ever pull that duty. Each time you take one of their things to hand it's like a punch in the solar plexus.

Neither at the wake nor the funeral did my father and I have anything further to say.

Back in California it took time for me to get re-focused on my career. The territory for my new sales job was the greater Los Angeles area. I was selling high reliability semiconductors utilized in satellites, commercial aircraft, radar and weapons systems. There were a lot of aerospace customers in the South Bay including Hughes Aircraft, TRW and Raytheon. Within a couple years I picked up additional territory and found myself covering most of Southern California. I had a great relationship with the majority of my customers and some became friends. I was an effective salesman, consistently finishing at the top or near the top every year. I also had a good relationship with the senior execs at the company, most of them old-school semiconductor guys. Crusty and cantankerous. My smart mouth and take-no-prisoners style was a perfect fit and within a few years I was promoted to regional sales manager.

Greater earning power made in-vitro fertilization more affordable, so I just gritted my teeth and followed the nurse's instructions when she handed me the plastic cup. The doctor was confident due to the quality of the embryos implanted and Tina and I had high hopes. But the process ended up failing. Shortly thereafter we had a follow-up appointment with the doctor.

"And how are we today?" he said cheerfully.

"I'm some thirty grand short!" I spat. "How about you?"

He seemed to sense my dissatisfaction. During our consultation he offered us a discount if we tried again. Under normal circumstances I would have told him where to get off, but at this point I was so worn down by the whole baby project that I simply agreed so as to avoid further discussion of the damn thing.

Let me write another check, jerk off into the cup, and leave me the fuck alone.

While we waited for this next anguished round, Tina decided she wanted to leave manicuring work. A client named Belle had said that her husband was starting an insurance business and needed part-time help. If Tina liked the new position well enough then she could transition out of the nail salon and sell her interest in it.

"Sounds great," I said. "You're too smart to gild nails all your life. You need something more challenging."

"I'm sure you'd like Alan," she said referring to the husband. "He's a macho guy like you. At least that's what Belle's always saying. He used to be a cop, you know."

"Just what I need – law enforcement."

She laughed, having meantime learned my family history. "It won't be just me and him. Belle works there too. Actually I think the only reason she suggested me for the job is she wants free manicures."

Tina's new stint seemed to be going well until one night when she came home upset. When I asked her what was wrong she made me promise not to react fearing I'd fly off the handle like in the gas-station incident. So I promised. Honest Injun. She said that Alan was on her case. Browbeating her for things she couldn't possibly have known, being new to the business as she was, and little mistakes that anyone might have made. I said I'd stick to my promise so long as she didn't bring her upset back home with her.

This would be the litmus test as to whether she could truly deal with the situation.

A couple weeks went by and all was cool. I was feeling not only proud of Tina but of myself for keeping my head so well. Despite my promise to her, my first instinct had been to throttle the guy. As it turned out, Alan's office was very close to one of the customers in my territory and I would drive past it a couple times a week. Each time with the temptation to pay him a visit. But maybe I was finally growing up, becoming a conscionable adult and law-abiding citizen.

The notion did occur to me.

Just when I thought this problem had been resolved, though, Tina came home in a real down mood. She didn't say anything but I got it out of her by remarking:

"Let me guess – Alan."

She gave an almost imperceptible nod.

I said nothing, letting it go at that, and surprised myself again by how calm I suddenly felt. But a scary calm. The die had been cast. I'd been absolved of my promise to Tina. And since we were about to start another in vitro, this guy would be stressing her out to the point that it might not only cost me serious money but someone to carry on the Costello name.

My gene pool was at stake.

Categorically unacceptable.

The next day, just before lunch and right after I'd finished a sales call, I paid a visit to Alan. His office was on Ventura Boulevard near Topanga Canyon Road. I went through the back entrance and up one flight of stairs. When I entered the office a woman stood up from her desk, presumably Belle.

"Can I help you?"

"Where's Alan."

She gave me no answer. But there was only one other person in the place, a man at another desk some twenty feet away, presumably Alan, and I made for him. He stood up. Tina had told me that he kept a gun in his desk but so far his hands were still where I could see them . . .

"I'll call the cops!" screamed Belle suddenly realizing I wasn't there to buy a policy.

"Try an ambulance," I said grabbing him by his lapels and throwing him against the wall. "Who the fuck do you think you are talking to my wife like that!"

There was fear in his eyes. I slammed him a second time and his body went limp. The window adjacent was open and I was tempted to throw him out since the awning beneath would have broken his fall. A herniated disc, a ruptured spleen, nothing too bad. And I probably would have done it if he'd offered more resistance. But the guy was a bag of bones. Still I felt like sharing my thoughts:

"Next time motherfucker you're going out that window!"

I gave him one last slam and as I strode past Belle's desk I couldn't resist giving her macho man a parting shot.

"I guess he's only tough with girls."

No more than fifteen minutes and I was paged by Tina. I debated whether to stop at the nearest phone booth. I knew a lecture was coming. I decided to bite the bullet. She tore right into me.

"This isn't Chicago! You could be locked up! There's something *wrong* with you – don't you understand?"

Needless to say the conversation had a sequel when I got home. She told me that Alan had threatened to call the police – this ex-cop certainly had his cronies – but that she'd gently informed him of my family history and offered that if he called his buddies then things would only escalate.

This was the one thing we agreed on that night.

The next day Belle came by Tina's salon with her severance pay.

Not unexpected. The surprising aspect was how shamefaced she was. Tina said Belle kept her head down and barely looked at her. Embarrassment that her manly husband hadn't turned out so manly after all? That he'd been thoroughly emasculated?

I like to think so.

Then our second attempt at in vitro failed. All this money and effort – and zero, zilch, nada! We discussed the possibility of a surrogate mother. But a surrogate mother combined with the cost of the procedure would be more expensive than what we'd already been paying out. I was making good money, but taking twenty and thirty-thousand dollar hits was now impacting our ability to trade up on our house. And if worse came to worst, having long ago given my family the middle digit, I had no buffer if things went south financially. You might wonder at all these economic considerations when the important thing was to simply have a child, to bring new life into the world, but until that child had actually *materialized* then these fiscal matters had a way of looming large and even taking center stage.

It was at this point that I began to resent my wife – and by extension my in-laws.

All my resolves to become a better man, to start a family and live down my father's legacy, were going up in a puff of smoke. Even when you tried to change, the fates conspired to slap you down. What was the use? You could bring all your powers to bear, all your willpower, but sometimes LIFE had it in for you. And I was neither strong nor wise enough to beat back my misdirected anger at this fact. I was reaching a point of resignation. The only thing I gave a shit about was that I didn't give a shit – because I knew the danger involved. There was this other world waiting for me, waiting with open arms, that world of faux glamour and ephemeral power and cheap illusions of grandeur. Tina had been a hedge against that world, against my own worst instincts, but now my feeling was that she'd betrayed my own best promise.

One of my coworkers at our corporate office in Santa Ana was getting married, so some of the guys decided to throw a bachelor party. We convened at this strip joint about a block from our manufacturing facility. After everyone else had left I hung out there playing pool while waiting for traffic to ebb for my seventy-five mile trek home. I noticed a guy staring at me. I ignored him for the most part until he approached. He was built like a Mack truck and just about as shy as one.

Name of Jake, from New York, which explained his attitude, he pointing at me and asking if I was a DEA agent. I told him to go fuck himself. That got a grin. We spoke for a good half hour. As it turned out we had some mutual friends from the wrong part of town. I told him I had to leave and he gave me his card and invited me to lunch to see his injection-molding business next time I was around.

We ended up good friends. He was affiliated with the Vagos Outlaw Motorcycle Club and over time introduced me to its members as well as the International President Terry "The Tramp" Orendorff. I went to several of their events and met bikers from other clubs too. I felt very comfortable at these affairs, I could be myself, let my hair down. If I was out at my corporate office, I would meet with Jake after work to kill time while traffic died down, like we'd originally met.

Jake was similar to me in that he straddled two worlds. Not only biker guys but he knew "high-profile" people in places like Bel Air and Beverly Hills. These ultra-rich types seemed to enjoy the tough but semi-polished exteriors that Jake and I projected. Per usual I wore tasteful Italian suits to work so that any event afterward I would fit in with all the other well-dressed people; Jake for his part never wore a tie, just a sport coat and slacks but lots of gaudy jewelry. Big diamond rings on fat sausage fingers. Maybe it made for an interesting contrast. All I know is that through Jake I started receiving invites to parties and other events from both the upper-class crowd and the biker clubs. Kind of a social teeter-totter. Now this, now that. Not half bad.

The problem was that Tina didn't fit in with either group. I wasn't going to bring her around the bikers and she wasn't enthused about the Bel Air crowd. She thought they were a bunch of phonies. And maybe they were. Though even phonies can be a lot of fun.

Sometimes the most fun.

But it was indicative of a deeper rift. It was getting to the point where I would sometimes forgo family events to attend the Bel Air parties. It was my way of avoiding the fertility issue and the increased stress I felt around my in-laws. No question about it, Tina and I were growing apart. Or in blunter language – our marriage had hit the skids.

Twelve

CONNUBIAL ABYSS

During the time that my marriage was disintegrating, my sister Margie was arrested and charged with illegal sale of a controlled substance (crystal meth) and with operating as a fence as well as being accessory to attempted murder. Nice! Late that night I received calls from family members asking me to bail her out, so I climbed from bed and drove the 45 minutes to Simi Valley where she was being held. After filling out the paperwork to post her bond the deputies brought her out and uncuffed her.

"Thanks Johnny," she said. "I didn't know if you'd come."

"Go out and wait by my car," I sneered. "And try not to fucking get arrested on your way there."

It wasn't long before Margie started her jail term at Chowchilla, a women's maximum security prison. This came less than a year after my father had finally been released from the pen. They were taking turns. I wondered who'd be next. My brother Bill had since become a cop, so he probably wasn't a candidate. By some miracle, in view of all my violent and otherwise questionable actions, I hadn't landed in the clink. Admittedly I'd had my share of luck. Which was bound to run out at some point if I didn't control certain of my less than admirable impulses.

And boy, was that control being tested now. Not long after, I was at a sales lunch and began receiving pages from Chicago numbers. My first thought was that someone was dead because that was typically the only time I'd receive pages from Chicago. I excused myself to find a pay phone and call one of the numbers. It turned out to be my old friend Marv Guccione. He tells me he's watching my half-sister and her mother on the Leeza Gibbons show and they're airing our family's dirty laundry. They are featured guests along with Antoinette Giancana – daughter of famous Chicago mobster Sam Giancana and known as the "Mafia Princess."

I asked Marv to send his videotape of the show by overnight delivery.

Viewing the tape the next day I was contemplating murder. Here was my half-sister and wicked stepmother[4] playing the victim card and telling half-truths and even outright lies about my father – stuff about severed fingers at the dinner table and other made-up garbage which was so outrageous that it doesn't merit repeating. Though actually it wasn't their shameless mendacity which I found so disturbing. By any standard my father had been no choirboy. But here were two people who had been living the good life while Billy and Margie and me were living in squalor, in and out of foster homes, while our mother – the true victim of my father's violence – lay dying in the hospital. This took some fucking nerve. I'd witnessed some rotten things in my life but this took the prize. These two self-proclaimed victims had lived in big houses, driven nice cars and had all the amenities and privileges of the upper middle class for years.

Furthermore, outside of vehement arguing or spanking at worst, nothing came close to the way we were treated.

4 Technically my ex-stepmother – she and my father had meantime become estranged – and all I could wonder was what took them so long.

There's the term "stolen valor" – when a person claims to be a war hero though having never even served in the military – and this was "stolen misery." These two people were attempting to hijack the very misery for which they were partially responsible in the cause of some sick type of fame and financial remuneration. I could excuse my younger half-sister because we had a good relationship and she had likely been unaware of our circumstance, but her mother knew only too well. Had the show's fact-checker placed a simple call to me, then both of them would have been discredited. My half-sister went on to do other shows like Geraldo, another guy I loathe, and Montel Williams, relating her tales of abuse, while my demented stepmother only appeared on the Leeza show, but that was enough to have reached a new low, even for her.

After watching the show I remember taking out my aggression on the heavy bag for five rounds. Then I worked the speed bag into a rhythmic frenzy while picturing my stepmother's face. This was equipment I had in my garage, which I'd turned into a makeshift gym. On Saturday mornings I would move the car into the driveway and have guys over and we'd work out and spar. Just fun stuff, me acting as their instructor, but then I heard that Newhall was starting a serious boxing program in its local community center. I immediately signed up as a volunteer trainer. This part of Newhall was predominantly Hispanic and many of the boxers came from the surrounding neighborhood. I loved working with these at-risk cases. Most were real good kids who just needed some guidance – and they were appreciative of the help we provided. Every so often I would slip one of them a few bucks for new boxing shoes or give them some of my old equipment. Most of the Mexican fighters had an aggressive style, always coming forward and cutting off the ring. This made for some intense sparring sessions. Visitors would drop in and say, "Jeez, I feel like I should pay admission for this." These guys didn't go half-speed. I enjoyed the same style and would throw down with some of the more experienced fighters and one or two of the trainers who still liked to mix it up. This gave some teeth to whatever I was telling the kids – whether it pertained to boxing or staying in school or keeping away from drugs. A guaranteed recipe for having some troubled kid listen to what you have to say is to just put the gloves on and show him you're not all talk. Our program was highly successful and over the course of time we produced dozens of regional Golden Gloves champions and even a couple national champions. World light-heavyweight champ Virgil Hill lived in the neighborhood and periodically stopped into the gym. Other professional fighters would swing by too. Consequently I was able to spar with several pros as well. The program was so popular that city officials would show up to our boxing events. I was something of an enigma to these guys – with whom I got along well – because the person they saw in the gym with gloves on his fists and tattoos on his body seemed a bit different from the professional businessman in his Armani suit at fancy restaurants and other high-profile city events and political fundraisers. They gave me looks like they were trying to place me.

Is that the guy from the community center? The dude who boxes with all the tough neighborhood kids? Nah, must be someone else . . .

Maybe these kids took the place of children of my own. Can't really say. But not being able to have a child was weighing heavily on me. It was causing not only a crisis in my marriage but a crisis of faith. After the second in vitro failed, I stopped attending mass with Tina on Sundays. Like God was sticking it to me, so what did I owe him? The in-vitro process itself clashed with Catholic doctrine. I had been justifying the procedure by rationalizing that God created science to help couples like us have children, but after the process failed the second time around I figured I'd gotten "mushed," which is an expression some of my wiseguy and outfit friends used to describe losing a bet because of what you might call bad karma.

Apropos bad karma – my wife's younger sister was going through a divorce. She was your typical Pollyanna, always seeing the positive side of things, but she had caught her husband philandering one time too many for the marriage to survive. She also had two young kids to deal with, so I gave her a hand by helping the three of them get into an apartment close to our condo. Shortly thereafter she began seeing a childhood friend who lived in Arizona. Although it was none of my business, this didn't go over well with me. I mean at least wait till you've signed the divorce papers before complicating your life. But the main reason was my own selfish thought that her new relationship would put any hope of her becoming our surrogate mother in jeopardy. She and Tina had discussed the possibility – and it would have been the perfect solution – keeping things in the family, as it were. But my sister-in-law said no. Which I completely understood. It was her body, she could do with it what she wanted, no question. But when her new relationship came to light, I felt it put a dagger through any prospect of her eventually changing her mind.

I had a heated argument with Tina. I'm sure I came across as an irrational jerk. But over the years my in-laws had come to me with various problems, and without going into detail, let's just say that I was uniquely qualified to handle them. And handle them I did – no matter how difficult the circumstance. So I was looking for a little quid pro quo. Flawed thinking to say the least. But I wanted to know all about my sister-in-law's new Romeo. Tina told me he'd had a kid out of wedlock from a previous relationship and that he managed his rich parents' general store somewhere in Arizona. He was middle-aged and had a history of drug and alcohol abuse.

"Doesn't sound like Mr. Wonderful."

"My sister thinks so."

"I mean the drugs and alcohol."

"He has it under control now."

"Yeah, until he doesn't again. Why expose her kids to that type of risk?"

"He loves her. She loves him. The best gift a man can give a woman's children is the feeling that he loves their mother."

"I'm gonna vomit! Where do you get this feel-good bullshit – from Oprah fucking Winfrey?"

I still had it in for talk-show hosts.

"No."

"What if she gets pregnant?"

Bringing up pregnancy was my way of expressing displeasure at her sister for not appearing terribly concerned with an issue that was destroying our marriage. I forget what Tina's response was; but I remember distinctly a few weeks later when she told me that – you guessed it – her sister was pregnant. Just another reminder how easy it was for others to do what we'd been failing at for years. Still I faced the music and helped her and the new guy pack up a truck to move to Arizona where they would be married once the divorce was final. I shook his hand and wished them both well.

While my personal life was collapsing, work was on the upswing. I had gained a reputation with the corporate executives as a performer. Additionally my customers were comfortable sharing information with me that they would never share with my competitors. Nothing unethical, just small things pertaining to timing and technical-application data. This gave me a tremendous advantage from a sales perspective. When I needed to make certain booking-numbers by specific dates, my customers would go out of their way to make it happen – sometimes even rescinding a substantial order from one of my competitors. These relationships allowed me great flexibility in not only managing my schedule but achieving my quarterly booking-numbers at whatever point in the quarter I found most amenable. This kind of efficiency freed up time for me to do other things like training fighters and hanging out with Jake, who as it happened was now getting married and who asked me to be his Best Man.

Tina and I traveled to Las Vegas to attend. Jake's wedding reception, at the Stardust Hotel, was needless to say unique. On one side of the room was Terry the Tramp with several of his Vago club members along with assorted other bikers and tough guys. On the opposite side were Jake's Beverly Hills cronies, including doctors, lawyers and corporate execs from the entertainment field. Neither side of the room mingled too much with the other, making me as Best Man the catalyst of the whole affair, a role for which I was eminently suited. And providing the entertainment? My father. He'd been granted permission by the Florida parole board to move to Las Vegas. He'd been able to justify the move because he had legit career history here singing in casino showrooms. Jake's reception wasn't a paid gig, but I'm sure my father's mouth was watering at the thought of being in a room with so many rich potential marks.

Jake had met my father previously. My father had driven to California with Eddie Caruso for some R&R, which in most instances would have meant reconnaissance and robbery, but it seems they were really here on vacation. I wanted to see Eddie, it would have been tough to give my father the brush off, and in any case we'd had a reconciliation of sorts at Gino's funeral. So I bowed to the inevitable and took them both out to dinner with Jake, who had already heard my father's records and been impressed with his talent and was ready to be charmed by him – which, as we know, my father was also good at. So when Jake was planning his wedding he urged me to put him in touch. What the hell. I viewed it as facilitating a contact.

At the wedding reception – as at the dinner date – my father and I weren't openly hostile to one another, but let's just say that our interaction wasn't the warmest.

On the other hand, Tina and I got along very well during the trip, which gave me hope that the marriage might survive – some weeks before, she had told me she wanted a separation. This news hit me hard and I expressed a desire to work things out. I even offered to go to marriage counseling, something I had always frowned upon. She agreed and we began attending sessions – separately. This struck me as odd but I was told by our woman counselor that it was perfectly normal and that after a few sessions we would have joint counseling. We were still going to these sessions separately when the Las Vegas trip happened, which as I said was going well, but the night before our return home Tina made a comment that made me think otherwise. Something about giving me up. I guess it could have been worse – "giving me up" could have meant she was going to testify against me in court for a criminal act. Still it wasn't really what I wanted to hear and succeeded in raising additional questions about our alleged marriage counseling.

That's when I decided to get to the bottom of things.

I was going on a business trip for a couple days, and since we were now technically separated I asked Tina if she would stay at our condo and take care of our German shepherd Storm. Before leaving I bugged my own phone hoping to find nothing incriminating on the tapes when I returned. But I did. There were a couple disturbing conversations between

Tina and an unlikely suspect – namely the older brother of my (still) sister-in-law's new husband. Did you get all that? Well, I got it like a bucket of ice water in the face. I had met this guy before and he was my complete opposite – coming across as mealy-mouthed and slimy.

I liked this guy slightly less than his younger brother, who I liked less than dysentery.

Rather than keeping my cool, I foolishly played my hand by calling his office, disguising my voice to the operator as she connected me with Steve. When he picked up the phone the first words out of his mouth were "Hello gorgeous!"

"Hey scumbag asshole, this is John, Tina's husband, and do you have any idea what I'm going to do to you?"

There was no reply.

I guess he didn't have any idea.

"So I'll fill you in," I said. "Tina and I are going to counseling and if things don't work out then the chips will fall where they may – but in the meantime if you don't stay the fuck away, I'll break every goddamn bone in your useless fucking body."

Still no response.

"Do you understand? Or need we go over things in detail?"

Again no response. This guy wasn't very talkative.

"Well, at least I'm clear!"

I hung up.

Now I planned on confronting the marriage counselor – this time employing my Eddie Caruso technique.

When I walked into her office for our scheduled session I took my usual place in the chair in front of her mahogany desk. Only this time I didn't greet her, just reaching over to the desk and picking up and examining her fancy letter opener. I started tapping its sharp end on the desk and said nothing, my eyes fixed on the blade.

"Is it something?" she said.

I stayed quiet, still toying with the letter opener, not looking at her. I wanted to ramp up the tension. I was doing a good job of it since I was even starting to scare myself. I finally raised my eyes from the letter opener and broke the silence:

"I have just one question."

"That would be?"

"Why are you such a no-good lying bitch?"

"You are making me feel uncomfortable, please move away."

"You know what makes me feel uncomfortable?" Now reexamining the letter opener, running my fingers along its blade. "When an alleged marriage counselor lies to me like I'm some kind of punk yuppie asshole."

"No one's ever spoken to me this way."

"Well, maybe it's about fucking time," I said, placing the letter opener back on her desk and now with both hands on the armrests of my chair. "Why did you string me along when you knew my wife was seeing this other guy? Why the charade? Is that in your professional code of ethics – leading someone down the garden path?"

She wasn't going to cop to anything, I knew that. Deny, deny, deny. And then I'd let her off the hook and walk out of her office and never return. No harm, no foul. But first I wanted to see her sweat a little . . .

"If you'll just tone it down a bit," she said, "then I'll be happy to explain."

Oh – hadn't expected that.

"I'm all ears," I said.

"First off the counseling is not always targeted at saving a marriage – some are beyond repair. That seems to be the case with you and Tina. At this point my job is to help you both through the separation and divorce process. Had we consciously approached things from that angle then you surely wouldn't have agreed to our sessions."

And you wouldn't have gotten your over-priced fee. I'd never heard such a crock. But I kept quiet, letting her try to talk her way out of things. It was actually pretty amusing the way she attempted to justify the bullshit she'd perpetrated.

When she was finished I stood up and walked out of the office, wordlessly, just as I'd come in. I'd gotten her confession, which was more than I'd bargained for, while also confirming my long-held feeling that her whole industry was a con game on par with the stuff my father had always pulled.

But in the days and weeks that followed – struggling through work and otherwise just moping around the house and taking long walks with my dog Storm – I realized that the counselor had been dead-on in one respect. Our marriage was over. It had officially lasted some ten years, but things had been going to pot for a long time now. And chiefly responsible had not been the infertility issue but my inability to handle it in a more compassionate manner. I didn't blame Tina for leaving me – I deserved to be left. Not that things could have turned out any differently, since I was dead-set on having a family, which would have been the source of endless frustration, but ideally I should have focused more on our marriage and not on the absent child. I shouldn't have taken each failure in this regard as a personal affront. I should have exercised greater self-control.

In short, I should have been a better man.

Maybe this was the first step to being one.

In any event a step it was – and time to keep walking and simply move on.

Thirteen

Return to the Dark Side

I was in the middle of a divorce and had achieved a state of anger rivaling my teenage years, which is saying a lot. My wife of almost a decade had essentially left me for an old boyfriend who was my polar opposite and represented everything I despised – a beta male with zero balls. There's no price you can put on affairs of the heart, but it sure didn't help that over the years I'd also blown a lot of money in trying to have a child with her. First infertile, then unfaithful, and me 30K-plus out of pocket. This can put a guy out of sorts. It can also leave your male ego pretty bruised. Consequently I lashed out at every opportunity to reestablish my masculinity. Not the most mature way to approach the situation, but nonetheless effective in helping restore my self-image as a man not to be fucked with. In short I needed to vent my anger. I was a 38-year-old single guy, no kids and no real family around to keep me somewhat balanced, and now I was about to enter a dark place where I didn't give the proverbial damn. During this time I would talk with my high-school friend Mark Richardson. Mark was keen-witted enough to realize that I was a walking powder keg and he did his best to prevent me from doing the draconian things of which he knew I was capable. But he was going up against a lot of personal history. For decades there had existed a battle between my head and heart. My well-honed instinct for self-assertion was in constant conflict with my sense of civility and was the cause of enormous stress. As a teenager I would imagine smashing my adversary of choice in the head with a baseball bat while spewing expletives until he was beyond hearing. But this fantasy sometimes failed to satisfy my aggressive urges, and real violence would finally emit. Though I like to think that it was never directed randomly. I had a certain internal code along the lines of Al Pacino's *in Scarface* – never doing anything bad to anybody who didn't have it coming – words to live by now as I reentered the underworld.

Back in the mid-1980s Eddie Caruso had taught me the fine art of loan-sharking. I also had a safe-deposit box and knew the going rate was six-for-five per week loaning money to mostly white working-class guys who couldn't resist blowing their paychecks on booze and table dances at blue-collar strip clubs. A couple of these establishments were located in the heart of the San Fernando Valley smack in the middle of my sales territory, and occasionally I would drop in, both with and without clients. So I'd gotten the lay of the land and discovered that these joints were ideal for lending money at high interest rates! By any practical standard this was very small-scale loaning. After all it was not the money that motivated me, I was already making good dough, but simply a way to satisfy my street urges and repair a damaged ego.

Of course these very same places were Hells Angel hangouts. I had met several club members over the years and we maintained a fairly cordial relationship. I did however have a couple confrontations with at least two "prospects" (guys who were candidates for membership in the club) and one with a full-blown "patch" (official club member) at an illegal after-hours party in a rented warehouse. This last incident along with rumored loan-sharking did not go over well with one particular Hells Angel member, a hard-ass Italian guy named Dominic Ferrara. He'd gotten wind of me and began making calls to New York City to check my credentials. I'm guessing he assumed I was making substantial money and wanted to muscle in if it turned out that I'd no official backing from anyone back east. But seeing as how I was from Chicago and only had Outfit affiliations, calls to New York weren't going to yield any street-cred, so Dominic believed I was fair game. As it pertained to California, however, I was associated with a couple other biker clubs, one being the Vagos where I had several strong relationships including with the club's international president Terry "The Tramp" Orrendorff. In those days the Hells Angels and the Vagos got along fairly well. Additionally I had become mistakenly linked to a separate operation (small book and executive card game)[5] with a couple connected guys from New Jersey and New York. When inquiries reached other clubs as well as my local associates, I was vouched for by at least three people. But this apparently didn't satisfy Dominic, and unbeknownst to me he requested a sit-down.

Jake and a guy named Sonny "D" represented me at this sit-down. Jake was of course my Vagos connection and Sonny was affiliate of a New York crime family. For the meeting both of them had to go to a Hells Angel hangout, in this case a pool hall, and listen to Dominic as he complained about my bad behavior. All well and good. That's what sit-downs are for – to air your differences. Then Dominic insisted on speaking to me directly. But it wasn't as if I could just hop in the car and swing by, since at the time I was vacationing in

---

5 "Small book" means petty bookmaking and gambling; "executive card game" refers to underground poker games where mob guys host and take a piece of the action.

Hawaii, trying to blow off some steam.

When I picked up my cell phone and Jake explained where he was and detailed the hostile company surrounding him, I blew that steam right up his ass and told him they could go fuck themselves. Jake told me to appreciate the situation and calm down. I managed to and then he handed the phone to Dominic and we conversed. Dominic's tone was calm but threatening. This didn't sit well with me. I tried my absolute best not to lose my cool again, but pride kicked in and Dominic responded by proposing that we should meet and settle the discrepancy face to face. Translation: he was calling me out.

Before accepting I suppose I might have given some thought to just who I was taking on. It was only after I'd hung up and made inquiries that I learned Dominic was a heavily muscled man of 225 pounds. I am all of 180 lbs. but did have years of boxing experience and always stayed in shape. Since I was still active as a volunteer boxing trainer at the nearby community center, I had the advantage of sparring several days a week with accomplished professionals and amateur fighters leading up to my showdown with Dominic. My strategy going in was based on the premise that Dominic would fight like other bikers I knew and simply use his size and strength to overwhelm his opponent. Most biker fights I had witnessed lasted less than a minute. My goal was to avoid any infighting so he couldn't get hold of me and to make him work so that if he did get hold of me he'd at least be good and tired. The longer the fight lasted, the better my odds of winning – not to mention simply surviving or escaping severe injury.

We met out in the Newhall area near a Mexican barrio. I had come alone, but Dominic was accompanied by an established martial artist whom I recognized. In sizing up

Dominic I began to think I'd made a mistake in taking this fight. The man had muscles in places I didn't even have places! Added to that, since the guy he brought along had serious credentials, I figured Dominic had some formal training and more aptitude than your average street fighter – so I may have underestimated his skill level. I watched him as he warmed up. He had a right-handed, open stance but fluid movement; big-chested so he would be slower to turn on his right hand, left hand strong but slow; weightlifter body so he would fatigue quickly. Don't get too close!

We shook hands and it was on. The adrenalin rush I typically experienced before a fight really kicked in but needed to be controlled. I couldn't afford to get wild and make any mistakes with an adversary this size. I started moving laterally to my right to avoid his power hand and to determine how quickly he countered. He didn't come straight at me in reckless fashion, which I had expected, but also moved laterally, a clear sign of formal training. Both his fists were closed indicating that for the time being he might be content to throw punches rather than grapple. As I had him moving to his right I stutter-stepped and landed a stiff jab just above his nose causing his head to snap back. He smiled and began coming forward in a more deliberate manner.

I moved left to gauge his reaction and he lunged forward with a right hand that streaked past my right ear while putting him off balance. I was in no good position to counter without the risk of getting too close and tangled up, so I kept my fighting stance and allowed him to right himself. Dominic stepped forward and threw a couple jabs followed by a right hand that caught me on the shoulder and nearly knocked me down. He had considerable power! Then he caught me with a left directly on the chest as I began my counterattack. But I could see his left was already slowing down so I continued forward and double-jabbed to his head, catching him on the second punch. He began throwing right-hand leads, so to take some of their sting away I threw open-hand left jabs at his right shoulder. This was an old technique used by Willie Pep and later Oscar De La Hoya to stifle an opponent's straight right. It also has a fatiguing effect on the right shoulder, especially if heavily muscled.

As the fight wore on I grew more relaxed while he began to press. I started landing consistently and could see he was becoming frustrated, which caused him to take more risks coming in. He could hit hard but was unable to land anything solid – though even those punches that merely struck my arms hurt like hell! This only served as further warning to avoid a clinch where he might take me off my feet. Then I caught him flush with a straight right followed by a short left hook to the head that stunned him, and I thought one good shot to the body and he was done. He was really hurting, possibly more from exhaustion, but the shots I landed certainly took their toll. He kept coming forward throwing punches but was clearly winded, and after I landed a couple more shots he hunched over as if to throw up. He'd pushed his cardiovascular system to its limit. There was no way he could continue. All told the fight had lasted five or six minutes. Once I came down from the intensity you experience during such an encounter, the pain began to kick in. Both my hands were brutally sore, there was numbness in my elbow and later in my chest and jaw, though luckily no major injuries.

I had to admire Dominic's tenacity and willingness to gut it out when things got tough. He certainly gained my respect, one for calling me out, and two for continuing to fight after absorbing some solid blows. We became friends after the fight and he invited me to several club functions. But just as this incident was closing out, another more serious one was about to emerge. My cousin Iron Mike and his buddy "Pipes" had come to visit me and I took them to some of the Hollywood hot spots and strip joints. Mike and Pipes were members of the Outlaws Motorcycle Club and were associated with both the north and south-side Chicago chapters. Mike was one of the toughest guys I have ever known, and though Pipes wasn't nearly as physical he was certainly willing to mix it up. Both of them had that stay-the-hell-away-from-me look and were very unapproachable. Consequently, every time we visited a club the security would politely request that I inform them if we encountered any problems with any other patrons and they would handle things immediately. They weren't saying this just to be nice – they were worried we might take matters into our own hands.

And there were in fact some tense situations. A number of the places we visited were periodically visited by Hells Angels. Although Dominic had given me entrée into the fold, the fact of the matter was that Outlaws and Hells Angels have a natural distaste for each other owing to a long history of violence between the clubs, so it is never a good idea to mix the two. Thankfully there were no incidents, but toward the end of their stay there was some trouble in a bar near where I lived. The place was called Rendezvous, a blue-collar joint that attracted some pretty rough customers. It was a "dive" bar everyone seemed to enjoy including me, and it wasn't long before I'd become a regular. The Rendezvous had a long oval-shaped bar from front to back. There was a jukebox and pool table and small stage for bands or a DJ. On the ceiling were graffiti-covered dollar bills memorializing certain of the bar's events over the years. On the walls were pictures of some of the patrons including memorials to several who had experienced untimely deaths.

Once a week they had "Bike Night," which attracted

bikers from surrounding cities. Rendezvous was also a stop during traditional biker activities like "poker runs" and other events in which Harley enthusiasts and full-patched club members would participate. It was a cold night and all three of us – Mike, Pipes and myself – wore the kind of black-leather jackets typically associated with New York or Chicago; in other words bristling with "attitude." We were minding our business, though, just talking among ourselves, when this young big-mouthed bitch decided to stick her nose where it didn't belong. We weren't really speaking loudly enough for anyone to hear us over the bar noise and music – maybe a loud laugh on occasion or an expletive that was blurted with a bit more volume than one would have ordinarily liked, but hell, this wasn't church or the public library but a biker bar. Anyway the first words out of her white-trash pie hole were: "You fucking guidos think you're so bad!" We were all stunned by the nerve of this broad, so I jumped in quickly and told her that if she didn't like our talk then she could go to the other side of the fucking bar. She began cussing us out and summoned her monster boyfriend. The guy approached in menacing fashion – easy to do when you're about six-foot-five – and his chin was immediately greeted by Iron Mike's fist. A crushing blow that sent the big man earthward. With precision and timing Pipes kicked him in the mouth on his way down to send a couple teeth sailing, while Mike grabbed the woman and gave her a slap which left a perfect impression of his hand on her cheek. This all happened in less time than it just took me to recount it. Since I was a well-known regular and big tipper, the bouncers peeled our victim off the floor and escorted him and his girl out the back door. When the bouncers returned, one of them told me we should probably split because the couple was going to try and flag down a squad car. The local cops were in the habit of cruising up and down the main road behind Rendezvous because of previous trouble that had gone down outside the bar. The place had a track record. The barmaid was a woman named Frankie whom I'd come to know, she was quite accustomed to this kind of violence, and she coolly poured us some tequila shots on the house before we scrammed.

When I returned to Rendezvous a week or so later, Frankie told me that we had gotten out of there just in time, sheriff deputies coming in a few minutes later with their guns drawn. When they questioned her about the guys who beat up the couple, she said she'd never seen us before and had no idea who we were or where we went. This time I bought *her* a drink.

The night before Mike and Pipes headed back to Chicago, I offered to pay for an upgrade of the car they were renting – it was a long drive and their vehicle was small and uncomfortable. When we arrived at the rental office a credit card was required for the upgrade and neither Mike nor Pipes possessed one, so I used my own card to complete the transaction.

Several days later I received a phone call from Chicago informing me of the arrest of the two in St. Louis, Missouri, on illegal firearms charges. These were not simply possession charges but federal offenses since Mike and Pipes were members of the Chicago Outlaws and had been found with suppressors, guns with the serial numbers removed, and a gun with no serial number at all. They could be charged under RICO (Racketeer Influenced and Corrupt Organizations Act). Not your average gun bust! And I knew that the authorities would soon be reviewing the rental paperwork and my name would pop up. It was only a matter of time before the law came knocking. I lived in a gated community, so in an effort to delay the inevitable I greased the guard at the entrance to have him inform me of any law-enforcement presence. If they asked for me by name the guard would respond that they had either just missed me or I was on some type of business travel and would be gone for a few days. This worked for months until the regular guard called in sick the very day that both the FBI and ATF came knocking once again. I had just returned from some customer visits and was in my garage retrieving my briefcase from my trunk when a pair of unmarked cars pulled up. As I grabbed the briefcase, the two surprise visitors approached while prominently displaying their law-enforcement credentials. The FBI man was a stocky sandy-haired guy, the ATF man a slender Polynesian-looking type.

"You're a difficult man to track down," said the FBI guy.

"Apparently not difficult enough," I said, walking down my driveway to meet them.

"Mr. Costello," said the ATF guy, "would you perhaps have time to answer a few questions pertaining to your cousin's visit to California a few months ago?"

"I have to write up my sales forecast for my region and it's due in a couple hours," I replied truthfully. "We can schedule a meeting once I've completed it. Give me your business cards."

"It won't take long," continued the ATF guy. "Just a short interview."

"You mean an interrogation – and I'm pretty certain it'll be anything but short."

But they were persistent and finally I asked them if they were prepared to arrest me and charge me with a crime, because if not then my career took precedence over their questions. When they said no, I promised to call them the next day to schedule a meeting. They looked exasperated but reluctantly agreed to my request. I took their business cards and went inside to complete my forecast and afterward devised my master plan.

As promised, the following day I called the ATF guy – Senior Special Agent Mike Halualani – and scheduled our "interview" at Denny's on Sepulveda in Van Nuys, a place directly across from a hotel frequented by prostitutes. I chose this locale because it was often a freak show full of distractions early mornings – the perfect venue to throw a young ATF agent off his game.

I arrived Saturday morning to behold a parade of scantily clad whores, a couple homeless guys begging for meals, and other strange walks of life – in fact it could have hosted a special episode of the Jerry Springer Show. When my adversary arrived at the restaurant he scanned this havoc of diners and finally spotted me at a booth in the middle of the establishment. As he sat down he cast one more glance at his surroundings and appeared intrigued by a woman at the adjacent booth wearing a modest pair of cut-off jeans that had half her ass hanging out. We shook hands.

"Nice place you picked."

"Only the best for my friends at the ATF."

He pulled out his files and began lobbing me some softball questions. Did you party with your cousin? What were the names of the clubs? When did you arrive? When did you leave? Whom did you meet up with? As he asked questions I would answer but also made a point of tossing the questions back at him to make it more of a conversation. I wanted him to feel comfortable, like he was speaking with a buddy. Since he was roughly my age, we had common interests which I exploited. Within minutes I knew where he was from, where he'd attended college, why he'd entered law enforcement as a career, and had garnered other information including what caliber firearm he preferred. I could tell he wanted to return to his script and each time he did I was able to decoy into another subject. I knew each question on his part was an attempt to corner me or get me to contradict some previous statement. A couple times in the middle of his question I pointed out some nice looking whore walking by: "Hey, check that one out!"

It was frustrating for him, but he knew exactly what was going on, a couple times shaking his head and grinning as he looked back at his report to get things back on track. In what seemed like a last-ditch effort he said:

"When your cousin was asked where he obtained the weapons, he indicated that he had received them from you."

I knew Mike would never have said such a thing. I looked Special Agent Halualani in the eye: "You know, I'm very disappointed that a guy like you, who attended a Jesuit school no less, should make such a false statement."

He looked down at his report again, but this time to hide his embarrassment. When he finally looked up he said: "I'm putting in a call to the Federal Prosecutor – I'll be right back."

I was hopeful the prosecutor would judge our informal interrogation as having miscarried, but when Halualani returned he apologized and reluctantly handed me the federal subpoena. My reaction was one of righteous indignation with some choice profanities thrown in – I was being called as a witness for the prosecution no less!

So much for my master plan.

I immediately contacted one of the premier criminal-defense attorneys I knew. Jim Henderson had defended several well-known organized crime figures including the Gambinos. I met with him in his office and discussed the situation. He gave me some very solid advice and told me to call him if there were any further complications.

The trial was in St. Louis in August, which caused me to miss the annual Crespi High School golf tournament! The trip was on the government's dime and I was given specific instructions where to stay upon my arrival; I was also to meet with the prosecutor prior to my court appearance. My attorney told me to make certain that I noted the exact time the plane landed in St. Louis because the feds were required to send me a "target" letter 48 hours after arrival informing me that I was being targeted by the prosecution – if such was indeed the case. This letter is a precaution by the federal government to make you fully aware of your Fifth Amendment right not to answer any questions on the witness stand that might incriminate you. Like a suspected crook getting Mirandized. All I needed. As I took my seat on the flight, I saw that the guy in the seat next to me was an acquaintance from the Rendezvous! Nice coincidence, I thought, does the government really think I'm that stupid? Sitting me next to a CI (Confidential Informant) and I'm not going to notice? Target letter or no, I was certainly getting the treatment. This eleventh-hour attempt to extract information from me was an insult to my intelligence. Suppressing my anger, I said a polite hello and then told the heavily tattooed gentleman that I seemed to be in the wrong seat; I then successfully changed places with someone a couple rows back.

When the flight landed I noted the time and recorded it in my Day-Timer. I jumped in a taxi and gave the Jamaican driver the hotel address. As we approached the hotel, the famous Gateway Arch loomed up as well as one of the sports stadiums – as if I needed any reminders, being a Chicago fan, St. Louis was home to the enemy!

I checked into the hotel and went to my room thinking it was bugged but really didn't care. For fun I blurted out: "If anyone is listening, go fuck yourself!" I cleaned up and changed into a nice suit. I had to go to the courthouse and take care of some administrative bullshit concerning expense reimbursement. It was a short walk from the hotel but in the heat and humidity it was miserable. On entering the courthouse I had to go through security similar to the airport. When I arrived at the federal prosecutor's office, I introduced myself to his staff through the clear plastic pane above the reception counter. They were very nice as they explained how I was to keep track of my per diem expenses. I told them I wasn't a "burger" guy and was planning on steak, seafood and rare vintage wine. They all laughed pleasantly as I signed the paperwork. The office manager was a middle-aged black woman who told me that the prosecutor wanted to speak with me and if I could remain awhile. I agreed and she sat me in a waiting area with this huge portrait of U.S. Attorney General Janet Reno looking down on me.

"Would you like any coffee or water?" she asked

"How can I hold anything down looking at that." I pointed to the Reno picture and the woman laughed and repeated her question.

"I'll have a water."

She left and brought it in a paper cup.

"Thanks," I said. "While you were gone I drew a fake mustache on the picture."

"You did *what*?" she said, looking at it.

"Just kidding, the mustache was there before I got here."

She was probably used to bad jokes by edgy witnesses and laughed good-humoredly. But after an hour of waiting and looking at that homely mug on the wall, my own good humor had evaporated so I left and had something to eat and didn't come back.

The next morning I was contacted by the defense attorney and we met straightaway for coffee in the hotel lobby. He told me my cousin Mike had accepted a plea deal and would do two years in prison, so he was only representing Christopher Metropoulos (Pipes). That surprised me about Mike. And this attorney must have done his homework because he knew certain things about my family. He was aware of my father's extensive criminal record. He knew my younger half-sister was a beauty queen (Mrs. Illinois) and had appeared on several talk shows in the mid-1990s. Surprisingly he also knew that her appearances on these shows greatly annoyed me and that I had contacted the producers and threatened recourse for things she had said. He was a nice guy and familiar with street nomenclature, using that language in speaking to me and not like I was some naïve college kid with a white-collar job. He told me he expected I would be called to the witness stand. I told him I'd see him during cross-examination and would try not to make fun of his ugly tie.

For the remainder of that day I waited in the hotel room, ready to go in my Armani suit, switching channels on the TV and periodically checking in with my corporate office. I ordered lunch from room service. Still no call from the federal prosecutor's office. Later I went out to dinner and then came back to the hotel room and crashed out early.

The next morning lying in bed I received the call. I showered, skipped shaving, climbed back into my suit, and headed to see Stephen R. Welby, Assistant U.S. Attorney. Again I waited in the same place staring at lovely Ms. Reno for over an hour. This time it wasn't the amiable black woman but someone less friendly. I told her I was going out to eat and would be back shortly. She asked me to stick around and it would be only a few more minutes but I said I had to eat now or I'd get a bad headache and then I left. Knowing that the 48-hour period for the target letter was about to expire, I had a more than leisurely lunch. When I felt I was home free I phoned my attorney for confirmation and he gave me the all-clear. The prosecutor was waiting for me when I returned to his office. He was a young guy with light blond hair who resembled Mayberry's own Opie Taylor more than the grizzled veteran prosecutor I had imagined. In fact he looked like he had just passed the bar exam. He introduced himself, reached me his hand and asked how I was. Knowing I couldn't be threatened with prosecution, and having experienced all their attempted trickery, I let him have it: "How am I you ask? I'd be on the back nine at Wood Ranch right now if it weren't for this fucking subpoena!" Not the answer he'd expected. His eyes widened and he invited me into his office. As we walked down the hallway I was already in his ear asking him where he went to law school and why wasn't he a criminal defense attorney since it paid better?

As we entered his office I noticed several guns in plastic evidence-bags on a small conference table. U.S. Attorney Welby took a seat behind his desk and next to him sat a man with a note pad who asked if I recognized the firearms. I was very familiar with guns and identified a 9mm Smith and Wesson, a 45-caliber Beretta, and a hammerless revolver that looked about 38 caliber but whose make I wasn't sure of.

"And here's a 15-round clip that's probably illegal," I added pointing to one of two clips in separate bags. "Sure I recognize these guns, I grew up on the street, but as far these *specific* firearms, these in the plastic bags, the answer is no."

They had me take a chair.

"That your family?" I asked before my ass hit the seat and pointing to a photo on the wall behind the prosecutor.

He gave me a laconic yes. He knew my game. I was trying to throw him off balance and he wasn't going to be thrown. But that wasn't my game at all. Not really. As we went back and forth, me interjecting all kinds of random and cocksure remarks, I just wanted him to get the feeling that I was a wild card capable of destroying his case. I'd wanted nothing to do with this business from the beginning, I was completely innocent of any wrongdoing, and I wasn't going to be a pawn in their game to convict a friend of my cousin. They'd already gotten Mike. After much verbal cat and mouse, the guy with the note pad asked if I could wait outside for a few moments. After I shut the door behind me I stayed there standing and kept my ears pricked. I caught snippets of the conversation. Basically they were concerned about putting me on the stand. My grand strategy had worked! There was just one hitch. My name was on the rental agreement for the car in which they'd found the guns. That fact couldn't be wished away. They had no choice.

Some grand strategy.

We finished up shortly after I reentered the office.

The next day I was called to the stand. After sitting in the witness waiting room for a period I then made my way to the courtroom to be sworn in. The judge sat on an elevated seat to my immediate right, the jury about ten feet to my left. The defense attorney and prosecution team were seated at a table in front of me. There were about twenty people in the spectator seats.

All eyes were on me. It's in moments like these when you became very conscious of how people might be perceiving you, and with my dark slicked-back hair, swarthy skin, brown eyes and shimmery Armani suit I must have looked like the prototypical Italian gangster. Not that this was a bad thing. Since my name was on the rental-car agreement, it was likely that the defense would try to deflect suspicion from Pipes by focusing on me as the guilty party. Since Mike had pleaded out, the defense could allude to some type of family conspiracy that would leave reasonable doubt in the minds of jury members as to Pipes' involvement.

The prosecutor arose and approached me on the witness stand and the questioning went something like this:

"What is your relationship to the defendant?"

"He's a friend of my cousin Mike."

"Your cousin Mike Ecklund who, along with Pipes, are members of the Outlaws motorcycle gang?"

The defense objected but was overruled by the judge, who instructed me to answer.

"Yes to the first part of your question, as far as the second part, I knew they were both Harley Davidson motorcycle enthusiasts."

"Mr. Costello," said the prosecutor as he placed the plastic-encased rental agreement, guns and silencer on a table in front of me. "Is that your signature on the rental agreement?"

"Yes."

"Mr. Costello, have you ever before seen the guns or the silencer I have placed in front of you?"

"No."

"No further questions your Honor," as he took the evidence-bags back to another table.

"Cross," said the judge in direction of the defense attorney, who in turn rose and approached the witness stand.

"Mr. Costello, please elaborate on how you are related to your cousin Mike."

"Mike is the son of my father's younger sister Arlene."

"Mr. Costello, you live in Los Angeles, correct?"

"Yes."

"But you are originally from Chicago, as is most of your family including your cousin Mike and your father, John Costello Sr. aka Mario Casini and Gianni Costa, correct?"

The prosecutor leapt from his chair objecting to the question but was overruled by the judge.

"Yes," I replied.

The defense attorney asked the judge to enter into evidence the plastic-encased letters he was now placing before me. "Mr.

Costello," he continued. "Is it true your father, John Costello Sr. aka Mario Casini and Gianni Costa is a known Chicago mob associate?"

The prosecutor raised an energetic objection and then asked to approach the bench. While he conferred with the judge I looked at the letters placed in front of me and realized they were angry protests of mine to the talk shows my younger half-sister had appeared on several years earlier. How he got them I'll never know. This painted me into a corner. If I responded yes then I'd be viewed as ratting, the lowest thing you could do, particularly where it concerned a blood relative. I'd be forever unwelcome in my Chicago neighborhood. Deny, deny and deny again! That's what I'd been taught. But a denial wouldn't have helped Pipes. And it wasn't like I wanted to defend my father – not after all the rotten things he'd done to me and my mother and my siblings. There was no call here for misplaced loyalties. I just wanted this problem solved by having the objection sustained. The prosecutor returned to his seat. The judge said:

"The witness is directed to answer the question."

"Please repeat the question."

I needed more time to think.

"Mr. Costello," said the defense attorney more emphatically and gazing in direction of the jury. "Is it true your father, John Costello Sr. aka Mario Casini and Gianni Costa is a known Chicago mob associate?"

I shrugged my shoulders and emitted a small but audible sigh as I leaned into the microphone: "Well, in the past the media has made those allegations."

Final result: Not Guilty.

The jury probably thought that I should have been sitting in the defendant's chair.

And here's an amusing postscript to the whole affair.

It was a year or two later that I received a jury-duty summons. I postponed service a couple times due to business travel but now I was required to appear. I showed up, filled out a form, waited around in a big room with other potential jurors for a couple hours and was chosen for the initial jury pool. Hadn't expected that. There must have been twenty of us selected and I was handed a badge indicating I was now juror number five. We then moved to an actual courtroom where a judge was seated on the bench. I glanced to my right and saw what turned out to be the defendant speaking to his attorney. He was a dark-skinned guy with black-rimmed glasses. We were directed to sit on staggered benches and then handed several pages of instruction. The judge told us the defendant was accused of distributing a banned substance, in this case crystal methamphetamine. The poor man's cocaine. Easily manufactured with most things you can find in a drugstore and fairly cheap. Not only had my sister been sent up for crystal meth but I'd had experience with "tweakers," or dealers in this poison, administering savage beatings to a couple of these parasites. I was only too familiar with this crowd of misfits and sat there thinking this must be a mistake. There is no way a guy with my background could be chosen to judge someone else in a criminal trial let alone for this particular felony. Don't they read those forms you fill out? Then the judge started querying each juror as to their respective questionnaire. The first few jurors appeared overly concerned about being related to an attorney or member of law enforcement, real minor concerns.

So now it's my turn. The judge asks which of the twenty questions pertain to me. I clear my throat and rattle off eleven of them. Stifled laughter from the jury pool, the judge a bit surprised, but he directs me to proceed.

"Well, first off, this guy" – I point to the defendant –

"looks like a tweaker to me and I have a sister who did time for that."

"You'll excuse my ignorance," says the judge, "but I'm unfamiliar with the term 'tweaker'."

"You know, your Honor, a meth head, a speed freak."

"Mr. Costello, would you care to approach the bench to discuss the other ten questions?"

"No need," I replied. "Most of these things are public anyway."

"Then please continue."

I did as instructed.

"My father is an alleged organized crime figure in Chicago and has been arrested numerous times, plead guilty to nearly a dozen felonies, done time in both Chicago and Florida and is still on probation. I bear the same name as him and it has caused me nothing but problems. I've been questioned by law enforcement including Federal Marshalls on multiple occasions. A couple years ago I was interrogated by the ATF, the FBI, and was subpoenaed to testify against my will in a RICO trial. Two of my cousins are in prison for drug offenses and two overdosed on heroin. You want me to keep going?"

By now the giggles are contagious and the public prosecutor is covering his mouth with his hand.

"Well," says the judge, himself visibly amused, "then I must ask if your negative experiences with the legal system will prevent you from exercising unbiased judgment in a court of law?"

"Whadda you think!"

The courtroom erupts in laughter – prosecutor, defense attorney, the works. The judge just shakes his head. I stay in character.

"Wha? Whud I say?"

I was summarily excused from the jury pool.

Fourteen

Ice Picks, Cigars, Hugh Hefner and the Pope

The company I worked for was growing to roughly $200 million per year in revenue and I had again been promoted. This time from Regional Manager to Area Sales Manager of a very large territory. At the National Sales Meeting I was awarded a plaque for "Most Aggressive Sales Person" – since they didn't have one for "Sales Person Most Likely to Serve Time in Federal Prison." My behavior was falling back into an erratic pattern – or make that a *frantic* pattern. I was playing catch-up. If not with others at least with my own personal goals. I wasn't anywhere near where I wanted to be after a decade of hard work – neither financially nor family-wise.

But there were some nice diversions. It was via Jake that I was able to meet and party with some of the LA "in crowd." Albeit somewhat reluctantly. After my divorce, in sync with my mood, I was more interested in hanging with a tougher and more reckless bunch. Then one night, just as I was ready to hit the sack, I received a call from Jake inviting me to the Rainbow Room on Sunset Strip. The Rainbow is an iconic rock-and-roll restaurant and bar in Hollywood where you never knew what famous actor, athlete or other celebrity might stroll in.

"We wanna introduce you to someone special," said Jake.

"Who?"

"I can't say."

"Why not?"

"I want it to be a surprise. Don't worry, you won't be disappointed. Now hop in your car and get the fuck over here."

"This better be special all right."

When I arrived it was as if the managers – Chicago guys I had known for a while – and doormen were expecting me. I was directed to the dining room's main table across from the fireplace. Per usual I scanned the premises, casing the joint, and saw no familiar faces. Except that of Mark Saginor. Dr. Mark was physician to some very famous people. We'd met at a few parties where he'd taken a liking to me. I walked toward his table. He arose and we exchanged greetings and then he took me by the arm and guided me back toward the fireplace table saying he wanted me to meet someone – and now I saw who that someone was. Hugh Hefner. I hadn't recognized him without his pipe and silk pajamas. Sensing my underlying agitation, though, which for months had been chronic, Dr. Mark whispered some fatherly advice as we made our way to the booth.

He was familiar with me and most of my family issues. He'd seen my sister's appearance on the talk shows. He had also met my father and Eddie Caruso and could clearly see I had never been provided any normal guidance from a male role model.

"Son, I know how you can let your temper get the best of you and I know what you are thinking of doing to your ex-wife's new boyfriend. Don't take the risk. Just let it go. In the end you will get what you want."

Then Mark sat us at the edge of the large booth where

Hefner was sitting. I knew Mark was his doctor but had never yet met the guy. As if on cue several of the people in the booth excused themselves, then Jake materialized and he and Dr. Mark shoved me down the booth till I was sitting next to Hefner. Dr. Mark introduced us and we shook hands.

"I hear you're from Chicago," said Hefner. "That's my hometown too."

"No kidding."

"The northwest side. Sayre Elementary and Steinmetz High. I wouldn't expect you to know them."

We talked Chicago for a while. The Chicago connection seemed important to him.

"I hear you're going through a divorce," said Hefner.

"Yeah, through the wringer's more like it."

He laughed. "I know how tough that can be. I'm going through a separation with my second wife. The best thing is distraction. You know, I'll be having some parties very soon and I'd like you to be my guest."

I was stunned. A personal invite from The Famous Man.

"Um, uh, uh," I stuttered uncharacteristically. "That sounds great – thank you Mr. Hefner."

"Call me Hef."

"Hef" told me they were going down the street to a "gentlemen's club" for a couple drinks and if I wouldn't maybe join them? I said I thought I could. They invited me to accompany them in their limo but I said I'd drive separately.

I had to catch my breath.

I liked Hefner's parlance – "gentlemen's club" – in layman's terms a strip joint. But a classy one. It also turned out that this certain club was being run by a good friend of mine, Kenny Coplan. As I walked through the place I saw a large reserved table roped off in a prime location by the stage. Kenny asked me to come backstage for a minute, saying he was sorry to hear about my divorce and then proceeded to a room where several women were standing around. When we came in they turned to us and all had big smiles on their faces – and that was about all they had on.

"Which one you want?" asked Kenny.

For the second time that night I was floored. But that's how Kenny was and why I'd always liked him.

"Well, ladies," I said to the half-naked bevy, "you're all lovely and I'm extraordinarily flattered, but I'm getting a divorce right now and not quite ready for all this."

On the way out I thanked Kenny for his gesture and went back to the table to join the party.

I'm an idiot, I thought.

After a decade of marriage it took some time adjusting to single life. But the Hefner connection would prove useful in this regard. A few days later in the mail I received the first of many invitations to a Playboy party. This initial event was not actually at the Playboy Mansion but another place every bit as impressive and owned by a guy named Lenny Ross, a Beverly Hills attorney. He had a limousine shuttle service, and as our chauffeur ascended the driveway there was something very familiar about the estate. Then it clicked. This was the house of the famous horse-head scene from *The Godfather*. If you remember the film then I needn't describe the place to you; if you don't, then suffice it to say it had every luxury imaginable – including its own nightclub. And the ratio of women to men at this party was at least three to one. *Beautiful* women. Not a horse head in the bunch. I'd always known that dazzling women and wealth went hand in hand, but this was like some kind of in-your-face demonstration of the fact. I was formally introduced to at least a dozen of these beauties and by end of the night I had a trove of phone numbers. There were so many numbers, and the women I'd gotten them from so uniformly stunning, that I couldn't keep them all straight in my head and began putting physical and other descriptions next to the names and numbers in order to remember who each woman was.

It got my dating life off to a decent start.

Then came the parties at the Playboy Mansion itself. Every few months I would receive a fancy invitation in the mail. The very first event I attended was "The Midsummer Night's Dream Party" – aka pajama party. It was a bit overwhelming. The women styled the sheerest of lingerie and sometimes only body-paint resembling lingerie. But it wasn't just the women at these events. You met luminaries in whatever field, often very interesting people – and the really famous ones, like the actors and rock stars, not so witless as you might think and with some pretty bright bulbs in the bunch. Halloween, New Years, Mardi Gras, Fourth of July – you'd see the same crowd and soon I became friends with several of these regulars. Scott Baio was one, he's told the story, and I also became close with a guy named Jimmy. At the time I only knew him as "Jimmy from Queens." That's how I greeted him – and he'd greet me as "Johnny from Chi-town." Turned out he was Jimmy Van Patten of the Hollywood Van Pattens. An accomplished actor and producer himself. Later I met his brothers and parents. Nice authentic people. Not at all Hollywood.

In the meantime my divorce proceedings were grinding on. Since Tina and I had no children and most of our savings had gone to in-vitro fertilization, outside of our condo and my company 401K, there were not many assets to split. So we determined it was better to reach an agreement without using an attorney. I'd been out Friday night with some friends at Barfly, a popular place at the time on Sunset Boulevard, and arrived back home around midnight, checking the mailbox on my way in. Among the half dozen standard envelopes was a thick one with a law-office return address. I opened this first. The letter was short and to the point, saying that there were irreconcilable differences between Tina and myself and that my financial records were being requested from the bank.

My future ex-wife had retained an attorney.

In our last conversation we'd explicitly agreed to come to terms without lawyers.

I was cursing as I opened the next letter. It was from her. Basically a candy-coated fuck you – apologizing for hiring an attorney to protect her interests. I was enraged but tried to get my mind around the thing. There was no way her family would have advised her to take this action knowing it would be viewed by me as a hostile act. But Tina on her own would have never pulled such a stunt either. Not Tina, not her family . . .

Her new boyfriend was behind this.

Though I had no proof. What I did have was this letter from the lawyer. They had dollar signs in their eyes – those mercenary bottom-feeders.

The lawyer.

I ran into the garage trying to locate our wedding album so I could burn it, but couldn't find the thing. But the wedding video! Aha! I grabbed it, jumped in my car and cruised the neighborhood until I found an open drugstore.

"Need an ice pick."

"Aisle four."

I returned to my car. I got the video and set it on the asphalt and began stabbing it with the newly purchased ice pick. $5.50 plus sales tax and I'd got what I paid for – the cheap fucking thing wouldn't penetrate the plastic. I braced the video on the side of a concrete parking stop. Crouched there in my Valentino suit, stabbing the videotape, middle of the night, cursing like a psychopath, I was the perfect candidate for a YouTube video gone viral. People were walking in and out of the store and giving me looks. It took some time but I was finally able to impale the tape on the pick.

When I got home I removed the ice pick, used it to skewer both letters, then re-stuck the whole mess onto the video. Back in the garage I found an appropriate-sized box and mailed things off to the attorney. Then I called old college pal and lawyer Jim Reiss and asked him to represent me in the divorce. Several days later I was at work when Jim rang me up.

"Johnny please – no more ice picks – no more insanity!"

But sometimes insanity can work in your favor. I had subsequent conversations with some of Tina's family members and it was decided that she and her attorney should back off.

At this point I was yearning for the forthright street justice I was accustomed to in Chicago. I gave a call to Eddie Caruso who updated me on my father's latest escapade.

You know Vic Damone, right? Frank Sinatra once said Vic Damone had the best pipes in the business but didn't have the know-how . . . whatever that means. So what happened was Mario's gonna headline this Italian Fest that happens every year in Chicago. All the Italian vendors come out, big crowds, nice entertainment. Mario's there to sing and a bunch of his Outfit friends there, too, along with Vic Damone. Apparently Damone was told that he could choose the guy who would close the show, right? But his agent says look, you don't want to put this guy in front of you cuz he's got a big voice and that big voice is gonna make you look a little bit . . . you know . . . diminished. So Damone agrees letting your dad sing last. What he does instead though, he finishes his last number and thanks everyone for coming – acts like it's the end of the show! People are getting up and leaving . . . show over. So my crew starts busting your father's balls. You gonna let him get away with this? So your father goes up on the stage and starts grabbing the instruments and throwing 'em

around, the musicians are screaming, and he just runs 'em out . .
. probably threatened to kill 'em or whatever. A big scene. And all
these Outfit guys laughing and watching your pop chase Vic Damone
off the stage. But it was chickenshit what Damone did, you know? I
mean you could understand why the agent told him not to sing after
Mario, it's not looking too good for you. So the crowd starts coming
back in . . . they're watching the ruckus . . . everybody wants to see
the train wreck, right? Your dad grabs a mic and starts singing, no
band, just a cappella, and the crowd comes pouring back in . . . it was
unbelievable . . .

Although my father was still on probation he was able to
move back to the LA area and start a new project. This time
– don't laugh – a religious one involving the Catholic Church
and Pope John Paul II. Hard to believe I know. But there was
method to his madness.

His scheme – I call it a scheme but there may have been
a molecule of sincerity behind it – was to claim he'd found
religion, changed his ways, and was seeking redemption. He
recorded an entire religious CD and through an old Chicago
high-school friend on the Pontifical Council he was able to
attain the rights to some exclusive Vatican footage of JP II's
visit to America, Mexico and the Philippines. My father's idea
was to play up his "redemption" and create a music video
using the exclusive Vatican footage and some of his newly
recorded songs.

I was not that tight with my father – I think that's been
established – but I thought this a great idea. And if he truly
wanted to be legitimate then I thought I might help him out.

But only on my terms this time. Which once meant giving
him a talking to.

It was a Christmas party at the home of Georgia Durante
in the San Fernando Valley. Georgia was originally from
Rochester, New York, and as a young woman became known

as "The Kodak Girl" due to the numerous times she posed as a model for Eastman Kodak advertising. At an early age Georgia was exposed to the mob world and later worked in Hollywood as a stunt driver – this all detailed in her book *The Company She Keeps: The Dangerous Life of a Model Turned Mafia Wife*. I had originally met Georgia through my father, who was also at the party, and I walked in to find him sitting at the same table as Henry Hill, the character Ray Liotta played in the movie *Goodfellas* who eventually becomes a rat. Hill was allegedly still in the Witness Protection Program so I had no idea why he was present at this party. I went over and whispered in my father's ear:

"You have to leave this table at once."

"Why?"

"Just do it!"

He stood up and I took him to one side and explained about Henry Hill.

"If you're seen sitting next to a government informant while on probation this will land you in hot water with both the good guys and the bad guys." The good guys were law enforcement and the bad guys were members of the Outfit. "This is a no-win proposition and I'm not covering for you if anyone finds out."

The next day Georgia e-mailed me some pictures of the event and among them was a photo of my father and Henry Hill. I called Georgia right away and asked her to destroy it. A few days later there was a feature story in the local paper including pictures detailing the celebrities in attendance at the function along with one snapshot identifying Hill in the company of . . .

Georgia.

The Kodak girl strikes again!

So we were spared one less headache. Matters were

complicated enough. My half-sister and unhinged stepmother's appearance on the talk shows had created a stir in Florida because people were outraged by some of the stories she told, whether true or not, and this had put pressure on Florida authorities to take action. As a result they would periodically haul my father back to prison on minor probation violations and he'd have to stay locked up until his probation hearing. I began feeling sorry for him. A first in my life. But here he was trying to go legit and being impeded every step of the way. They were truly harassing him. It stemmed from those trash talk shows. He was getting a raw deal. So I linked him up with a couple attorneys and helped him monetarily.

Over the last couple years I had been receiving letters from my older sister Margie who was serving time at Chowchilla, a min-max woman's prison in Central California. My sister has always been rough and able to handle herself, and not surprisingly she had already been in a few scrapes and established a reputation among the other inmates as someone you didn't want to mess with. I always wrote her back and would include photos of me with celebrities at the Playboy Mansion. What a mistake! She shared these pictures with her prison friends and soon I began receiving mail from them along with photos and proposals that were pretty explicit. And I thought guys could be crass! As my sister's release date approached, the revolving door continued when my cousin Iron Mike readied himself for his jail term. I would be heading to Chicago to organize his "going away party" – as such things are termed in criminal circles.

Interestingly, I was able to use these bizarre circumstances to my advantage career-wise. I had become familiar enough to my clients that they could sense if I wasn't quite myself during our interactions and they would ask me if anything was wrong. I didn't want to lie so I provided some of the sordid details – which were hard for me to articulate without using rougher language. I would temporarily set aside my professional demeanor and transition into "street mode," explaining the situation in the manner of characters from a movie like, well, *Goodfellas*. It had taken me years of discipline and practice to avoid sharing this side of me, but now it was emerging as beneficial. Many of my customers were highly educated engineers and business professionals who were unaccustomed to hearing such offbeat and even aberrant tales from one of their top-tier suppliers. When we were done with the business at hand they would close their office doors as I launched into accounts of my latest rendezvous with lunacy. I shared most everything – pictures from the Playboy Mansion, videos of my father, prison letters from my sister's fellow inmates, federal subpoenas – it was equivalent to a reality soap opera and every sales visit was the next episode. Being able to openly communicate to those in my white-collar world helped me accept myself for who I was without judgment or stigma. This was liberating to say the least. And my clients seemed to be enjoying themselves.

I continued attending events that were polar opposites in terms of the human element, but sometimes these worlds would intersect. A friend from the Playboy Mansion was being harassed by some drug-dealing "tweaker" and through a third party asked if I could help. Since my sister and outlaw biker friends were familiar with this world, I was able to locate the tweaker, a guy named Jesse. I had a personal distaste for drug dealers and wanted to confront this scumbag myself. I was told Jesse had a wooden leg. My plan was to knock him on his ass, pull his wooden leg off and beat him with it – just for the comedic value. After several failed attempts to find Jesse at various strip clubs, I was finally able to isolate him in a residential area in Moorpark. I parked my car on a cross street and walked around the block waiting for Jesse to arrive at a house where I knew the occupant would not be home. I wore a baseball hat pulled down over my eyes, jeans and a baggy shirt. I saw a guy sitting on the hood of a car directly in front of the house. He resembled actor Keanu Reeves only skinnier and with bad teeth. He watched me suspiciously as I approached and came down from the hood but didn't assume a defensive posture.

"How ya doin'," I said.

"Who are you?"

"That's not important, what's important is you stay the fuck away from Rachel."

"What's it to you?"

I gave him a hard slap but not that hard. I'm guessing the wooden leg caused him to easily lose his balance – at any rate he hit the ground. I grabbed his leg and began pulling and he was shouting to get off him. It seemed like a real leg so now I'm thinking I either have the wrong leg or the wrong guy. Just as I was going for the other leg a couple cars slowed down so as not to hit us – or just to get a ringside seat at this farce. I thought it was time to leave. I told Jesse:

"You've been warned – don't make me come back looking for you!"

He didn't. Though a low-life sleazeball, Jesse was smart enough to ask around his biker contacts and realized that he'd better heed my warning.

I still wish I'd gotten to beat him with his own leg though.

I shared the tweaker encounter with Sonny D and Lou Ipps and some of the other guys that hung out at Albano's Pizzeria, which was on Melrose in Hollywood. Albano's had excellent food and was a very popular place. The owners were brothers from New York and well connected themselves. Besides the restaurant, they ran a catering business that served the entertainment world, so a lot of celebs would end up visiting their restaurant. Albano's was also a hangout for many displaced wiseguys from Boston, New York and New Jersey. It was almost like a sidewalk Italian social club. I had originally met Sonny D through my father. Sonny was a Hollywood stuntman, a well-built and intimidating man with a hard edge. Sonny could be extremely volatile when someone or something rubbed him the wrong way – but this was balanced by a great sense of humor. The trick was to get him on his good-natured days. It was Jake who introduced me to Lou, who was a street-wise New Jersey guy. He reminded me of actor James Gandolfini from the HBO series *The Sopranos*. Lou wasn't as beefy as Gandolfini but he carried himself in the same confident manner – the kind of confidence you get when your father's also a capo in the New Jersey mob. Both Sonny and Lou were about ten years older than me and both had done time in prison. They told me riveting stories of the old days and their experiences, which had the effect of making me feel that my life, in comparison to theirs, wasn't that outlandishly violent and crazy after all.

It was me who introduced the two. They eventually got together and opened a cigar lounge called Da Big Smoke right next to Albano's Pizzeria. Da Big Smoke was more than just your average cigar lounge because in the back was an executive poker game and a small bookmaking operation. After grabbing some Italian food at Albano's, patrons would head to Da Big Smoke for an espresso and a cigar. At the time there was a lot of street traffic on Melrose, so both places were very busy. Many stars would come in, seeming to enjoy the wiseguy atmosphere; other celebrities dropped by simply because they were long-time friends of Lou and Sonny – people like singer Frankie Valli and actor Joe Pesci. Lou not only introduced me to these two gracious men but took me to their San Fernando Valley homes on a number of occasions – for instance the Sunday Italian cookouts at Joe's place and the chef's role being played by another New Jersey friend Johnny Nardone, who operated an Italian restaurant in my neighborhood. Joe also owned a racehorse (with the imaginative name "Joe Pesci") and we'd go to Santa Anita and bet and watch his horse run. Periodically we'd meet at the Amazon Restaurant on Ventura Boulevard or at Mastro's Restaurant in Beverly Hills, finishing off with cigars on the terrace. Or I'd host a pay-per-view fight at my place followed by cigars in the backyard with Lou and Frankie Valli. But Thursday nights were always reserved for Albano's, often with Scott Baio, and then we'd head to Da Big Smoke for the ceremonial after-dinner cigar.

We liked our cigars.

Fifteen

Executive Decision

Being single freed up much of my time and I took full advantage by hanging out with the guys. One of these was Dino Guglielmelli. He ran a small manufacturing business specializing in vitamins and supplements. He was good-looking and good-tempered, not a macho guy by any stretch, but he'd been to the Playboy Mansion several times and so it was by virtue of this connection that we'd a number of friends and acquaintances in common. What we also shared was an enthusiasm for hockey. Dino had season seats for the L.A. Kings, so whenever the Chicago Blackhawks were in town he invited me along for a game. It was through Dino that I started back on collecting bad debts, he giving me a 50-percent commission, which I mention because it sort of got me primed and in training for my next little episode.

Lou Ippolito had a close associate in Las Vegas named Danny Walsh whose colleague had gotten in deep with a local bookie named Leo. The debt was eventually paid but Leo was asked to stop taking bets from the colleague. Of course he didn't. A new debt of 80K built up and that's when Lou along with Sonny D asked for my assistance. Usually I was on the other side of the equation, but I was happy to help in any way I could.

First thing was to meet with Leo. That initial encounter he came with his heavy – an imposing dude named Mike who had been a pro tight end. Leo was a good-size guy himself as well as being confident verging on cocky. He provided names of the people he was "with" – presumably those connected individuals who would back him since they were being paid a *vig*, or tribute, basically guys who were protecting him from guys like us. Like good businessmen we did due diligence by meeting the people he said were "with" him, but as it turned out no one was with him. None of them were willing to go to the wall for Leo. He was on his own, thrown to the sharks.

Lou arranged a follow-up meeting with Leo and his heavy Mike at the Amazon Restaurant. Breaking the bad news to Leo were myself, Jake, and Danny's younger brother Chris. Christopher Walsh was a tough kid who like myself had trained at Broadway Gym, so we had lots to talk about. Sonny and Lou made me point man for the negotiation, and prior to this second meeting I called Steve Cuccio who owned the Amazon and asked him to remove the videos from his security system, which he obligingly did.

In arriving at the Amazon we found Mike near front of the restaurant in a chair facing the window. We shook hands and then the three of us took seats directly across from Mike.

"Where's Leo?" I asked.

"He's on his way," said Mike.

Chris had a murderous look in his eye; clearly he wanted a piece of Mike. Jake just sat there staring.

"Tell you what," I said, "I'll start this show. Our guy will pay you fifty bucks a week. That's our offer. Now where's Leo."

This was the equivalent of saying shove the debt up your ass.

"Wait," said Mike. "That's not fair."

"I didn't say it was fair, I said that's the way it is. Am I going to have a fucking problem with you?"

I doubt Mike was expecting this full frontal assault. The reality was we were prepared to severely beat both him and Leo – right there in the restaurant if necessary – and I believe at this point it was sinking in. Mike began frantically texting.

"What about all the names we gave you," he said as his thumbs twitched up and down. "Didn't they check out?"

"Your own people hung you out to dry," I replied. "What the hell are you doing?"

"I'm telling Leo not to come, I'm not bringing the lamb to the slaughter."

It was going to be a short meeting. At this point my main concern was just keeping things cordial and preventing Chris from going over the table at Mike. Then Mike completely backed off and the tension dropped. We actually exchanged contact info and left on good terms. Mike mentioned he was an Executive Host at the MGM and said he'd take care of us next time we were in Vegas. He was all right. Then again I've always liked a guy who can settle out of court.

About this time I began dating a woman named Janell. When I first laid eyes on her she'd been dressed as a canine. It was at the Playboy Mansion's annual Halloween party and she was wearing a light-blue poodle costume. Tame by Playboy standards but still leaving little to the imagination. Janell was a print model, not a Playboy Playmate, a gorgeous brunette with dark brown eyes and a knockout figure. I was dressed like the devil with red horns protruding from my forehead and a pentagram on my chest.

"Excuse me," I said as she jiggled by. "I'm from animal control and will have to take you in for not having tags."

She stopped with her hands on her hips and looked me up and down.

"Do you perform tricks?" I continued – then realizing my double entendre: "Sorry for my brazenness but I am the devil."

She laughed. Thankfully. Conversation followed. We stayed talking for quite a while – and agreed to see each other again.

"How about tomorrow," I said.

"Tomorrow?"

"Why wait."

"You *are* a little devilish."

At lunch the next day, both of us back in our civilian gear, we really hit it off. Janell was working full time and studying at Cal State Northridge where she was about to earn a degree in finance. Just speaking with her I could tell she was an extraordinary person. Super smart and ambitious – my type of woman!

For my cousin Iron Mike's going-away party I called many of my friends and relatives to make certain they would attend and bring an envelope with money to defray Mike's bills while he was in prison; this was a traditional practice. One relative who didn't show was my first cousin Lisa. I'd always liked Lisa, a nice pretty girl when younger but who then started running with a scumbag crowd. It had been sad to see her steady demise. To support her drug habit she started working as a prostitute – and I don't mean one of your high-priced call girls but a bargain-basement streetwalker. Recently it had looked as if she might defeat her demons, having obtained a job at a dry cleaners and attempting to get her life in order. She was 38 years old with a couple of kids – so it was long overdue. But now she had relapsed into drugs and drifted back into walking the streets. Later she would be pinched on a prostitution sweep, and the day of Lisa's release she scored some heroin, apparently not realizing that her drug-free time spent in jail made her body unable to handle the dosage, and she was found dead in a cheap hotel room with the needle sticking out of her arm.

But my father and sister Margie both made it to Mike's party. They were no longer in prison though on parole, the terms of which stated that they couldn't associate with other convicted felons, so they needed special dispensation to attend. Iron Mike was not only a convicted felon but a known member of the Chicago Outlaws and sergeant-at-arms (responsible for discipline and security) of his neighborhood chapter. The party was at a bar outside Chicago in Northbrook and there were both marked and unmarked police cars in the parking lot. Another rough character in attendance was Anthony Palermo. Tony was part of my "extended family" – not a blood relation but a guy who still had my back – and he enjoyed a ferocious reputation. Just prior to performing demolition on someone foolhardy enough to challenge him, he would proclaim he was 99-0 in street fights so why not make it an even hundred? I always got a kick out of that line. Tony mentioned he would be visiting Los Angeles soon and we should get together. He wanted to take me to see Johnny Fratto who had moved to Beverly Hills. Johnny was one of the guys who broke my balls fifteen years earlier for my brawl in the Viking restaurant. I had not seen Johnny in a long time so it would be nice to catch up.

What I first noticed in meeting again with Johnny was his full head of white hair. The last time I'd seen him it had been salt & pepper – mostly pepper. It was my turn to bust his balls. Our reunion was a good one. Johnny told me to come by and see him next time I was in Beverly Hills. In the years to come I would end up stopping at his house about once a week for lunch on my way to or from sales calls in the south Los Angeles area.

Now a couple things about Johnny. First off is that his father was Lew Farrell aka Louis "Cockeyed" Fratto, a guy in the upper echelons of the Chicago Outfit since he worked directly for Al Capone. So Johnny had more than a little street-cred – if merely by association. The other thing was Johnny's ability to self-promote. He became a regular on the Howard Stern Show and appeared on several other programs as well. His current celebrity stemmed from an incident involving Paris Hilton and Kim Stewart at a Maxim 100 red-carpet affair. Johnny had a company called Beverly Hills Choppers that built "mini–choppers" – small decorative bikes – for the rich and famous. On this occasion both Kim and Paris were revving the engines of their mini-choppers while on the red carpet and with cameras rolling when Kim accidentally released the clutch and the bike shot forward and she hit the deck. This video must have played thousands of times on different TV stations globally and was covered by all the tabloid magazines. There was talk of a lawsuit until some of those same tabloids revealed Johnny's mob legacy. This not only made for additional tabloid fodder but it gave Johnny and Beverly Hills Choppers worldwide fame. Using his God-given promotional skills, Johnny eventually attained something akin to cult status – and out of that came two reality-show pilots based on the Kim Stewart incident and called "Son of a Gun." Johnny asked me to appear as a main character in both. I told him I didn't even know how to act at home, just ask my ex-wife. Sonny D and I ended up in the first pilot and Jake and myself in the second one. It was fun but never went anywhere – so my obvious lack of talent would stay safely under wraps.

A couple other things about Johnny – he was a chain-smoker and deathly afraid of flying. This second foible had more than a little to do with the fact that his brother Frankie had been killed in the very same plane crash that took the life of heavyweight boxing champ Rocky Marciano. So when one of Johnny's close relatives passed away it was me who was tasked with holding Johnny's hand on a flight from Los Angeles to Chicago. When I got to LAX and walked into the terminal I immediately spotted him – not only because he was hard to miss with his snow-white hair and excessive gold jewelry, but he was animatedly arguing with an agent from the Transportation Security Administration. Turns out he'd been smoking in the terminal. And was still smoking. Defiantly so. I told the TSA guy that Johnny was upset about a death in the family and then whisked Johnny away while grabbing the cigarette out of his mouth. Seems Johnny had also tanked up on Xanax so he wasn't all there mentally. We make it to security and the first time through Johnny bumps the side of the metal detector and it goes off. He bumps it again on the way back, setting it off once more. And a third time – because of something he's wearing. Not his jewelry. That's all been placed in the tray. They take him aside for one-on-one screening where he promptly reaches into his pocket and pulls out a lighter to try and light a cigarette. Guy couldn't part with his precious lighter. Fucking nightmare as I keep trying to explain that Johnny's erratic behavior is due to his being so distraught. So we ditch the lighter and they finally allow us to board the plane. As soon as Johnny and I are seated in first class, I ask him for his pack of cigarettes since I suspect he might have snuck matches in his carry-on. He has the window seat and I have the aisle, mainly to keep him penned in and not get up and do something crazy. We're still on the tarmac but Johnny is sky-high from the Xanax when he puts on his head phones and says: "I'm not even here." Yeah Johnny, that's been pretty clear for a while now. When we arrive at O'Hare Airport I escort him to ground transportation and then release him into custody of a mutual friend who must have had cigarettes on him because after walking away I take a look over my shoulder and see Johnny lighting up. Or maybe the pack he'd given me was only a decoy – more than likely . . .

In my line of work you can be doing extremely well at your job, but any shakeup at the CEO level can change not only your career path but also mean losing your position. It was about this time that rumors swirled as to the imminent retirement of the man who was the original founder and major shareholder of the company. He was a veteran semiconductor guy who had succeeded in purchasing many companies but never consolidated them effectively, thereby resulting in poor factory utilization, sales conflicts, high overhead, redundancy and above all poorly performing stock. He was a great engineer but not someone focused on Wall Street and shareholder value.

I was notorious for berating the Divisional Sales Managers of New Acquisitions whenever I disagreed with what I thought were poor policies. I hated when some bullshit divisional policy or administrative rule prevented me from making the magic number guaranteeing my bonus. Many times I would call the Divisional General Manager and hammer him in order to achieve that bonus. Sometimes I was too aggressive and would then be called up in front of the CEO. Waiting to see him in the boardroom was like sitting outside the principal's office but with higher stakes. Whenever the Executive Secretary saw me sitting there she would ask: "What did you do this time?" After pleading my case the CEO would mostly side with my reasoning – or pretend to – but there was one time when I thought I might have gone too far.

Jimmy "P" was GM of one of the company's latest acquisitions and he and I had a short but spirited confrontation on the telephone. To conclude the conversation we agreed to a meeting to "straighten things out." Which may sound pretty harmless but the whole undercurrent of our exchange was hostile. Then within a week of this spat I received a courtesy call from the CEO informing me that he was stepping down and wanted to tell me personally since I was a long-term employee. Then came the topper – he was appointing Jimmy P the new CEO. Oh well, I thought, time to dust off the old resume. My fate was sealed. I gave Jimmy P a call.

"Just wanted to congratulate you on being appointed new CEO."

"Thanks John, that's very sporting of you."

"I guess this will change the tone of our meeting next week."

Jimmy laughed but I knew how the corporate world worked and that there was a 90-percent chance he would replace me with one of his own people within months of his assuming the role of CEO. It was clear that drastic changes were underway. Everyone would now be competing for jobs because redundancy was to be eliminated and factory utilization and integration made top priorities. And sure enough, after Jimmy P officially took over he began canvassing all the current corporate sales managers. I was one of the last to be interviewed. Since I figured I was going to be fired, I decided to be brutally honest and direct. Jimmy's first question was:

"How many hours do you work on average per week?"

"About twenty – depending on where I am on my sales goal."

Most guys would have said anywhere from forty to sixty. We talked some more. Then Jimmy picked up the phone and called Ralph Brandi the Chief Operating Officer.

"Ralph you need to come in here," said Jimmy. "I'm

talking to the first honest sales guy I ever met."

When Ralph came in I repeated what I'd told Jimmy – that I met my sales goal roughly halfway through the quarter and the dysfunctional sales model penalized me if I went over my goal, so why work more to make less? I also pointed out several flaws in the sales policy and structure that I had brought up in the past but which had been ignored by my direct supervisor at the time. During this conversation my well-groomed corporate demeanor gave way to that straight-talking Chicago kid inclusive off-color language. What did I have to lose at this stage?

A week later when Jimmy P called me into his office I thought it was to let me go. But to my amazement Jimmy P fired most of the other sales managers while keeping me on board. His logic was that if I could pull those top numbers in a twenty-hour work week then what might I do working forty hours per week with the proper incentives? Jimmy handed me a large notebook and asked how I would restructure the domestic sales force if I were in charge. When I expressed reservations as to what my boss might think, Jimmy used a line straight out of my own repertoire: "You let me worry about your boss."

I knew then that my boss was going to be a casualty.

Within days I had submitted a detailed plan to streamline the military/aerospace sales force. Not only did the plan provide maximum sales coverage to our key accounts at a minimal cost to sales but it also provided a mechanism to increase bonus pay. A few months later my plan was adopted and I was promoted to Director of North American High Reliability Sales. In the process I had many meetings with Jimmy and Ralph and learned how they were going to repair and grow the company. They were on the verge of making some very daring decisions that would shake up our industry, and I was excited to learn that I would be point man in the execution phase.

I spent more and more time with Ralph and Jimmy and got to know them extremely well. Jimmy P was from New York and had an edge to him that I liked. Ralph was the talented, cantankerous, Pall Mall-smoking operations guy. Both these gentlemen had my undivided attention and respect. I began to bear down at work, forsaking just about everything else. The company was growing and the stock skyrocketing. Jimmy and Ralph's plan was working better than imagined.

That said, I had opened-up to Jimmy P and he knew some of my family history and the crowd I ran with, mainly due to social events where family and extended family invitations are difficult to avoid. With this knowledge in hand, after I was promoted to a Corporate Director, he warned me of the risks I presented to myself and the company while indicating that I had a bright future. "So don't fuck it up!" he told me – again in my native tongue.

At one point I thought I might have.

It was after an all-day sales meeting cooped up in a board room and buttoned down in our three-piece suits. After dinner we all went to a place called the Shark Club, a high-end pool hall, and Ralph and Jimmy came with. To make a long story short, some dickhead decided he was going to play rough and try to intimidate all these tie-wearing business types who had just crashed the club. Within seconds I'd called the guy out in an expletive-laden tirade as I walked toward him. A couple patrons jumped between us as I challenged him to go outside and then made my way to the door while continuing to bait him with insults. Then I noticed Jimmy and Ralph right behind me. There goes my career, I thought, they gave me one big break but no way I'm getting a second reprieve. I turned to Jimmy.

"Sorry boss, the guy was bullying the sales team."

"Don't worry," said Jimmy. "We're standing by if anyone else jumps in."

There was no need to since the douchebag backed down, but now I knew I loved these two guys!

When we completed the restructuring of North America I was tasked to do the same for Europe, which took me several months. Then they put me on Asia. I was doing extensive traveling and had my nose to the grindstone. It was imperative that sales meet our quarterly numbers to keep Wall Street satisfied. About halfway through the Asian effort, Jimmy P poked his head into my office late one afternoon and said he was going to "take care of that thing today." I looked up from my desk and said okay, not really knowing what he meant. Shortly after 5 pm one of the Executive VPs came to my office and invited me to dinner at Morton's Steakhouse. We ordered cocktails and then my colleague pulled out a file and congratulated me on being promoted to Corporate VP of Global High Reliability Sales. Something completely unexpected since I had been promoted to Director only a year before. When I reviewed the file – especially after seeing my new compensation package and benefits – I was filled with a euphoria I'd never before experienced. On my way home I called Jimmy P to thank him. He replied that I'd earned it and then said something no grown man had ever told me before.

He said he was proud of me.

In 43 years I'd never heard anything approaching it. Not even an "attaboy" or a pat on the back. Not from my father, not from my grandfathers, not from my uncles, not from any male member of my family.

After we ended the call I got a little choked up.

Some tough guy.

Sixteen

Knowing I had so much to lose by fouling up, I was now finding it increasingly difficult to balance my worlds. But sometimes it worked out. There was a VP-level representative from one of our major distributors in town. Frank Stalzer was a New York guy with a New York attitude. I invited him to dinner at Mastros in Beverly Hills and asked my friends Scott Baio and Jake to join us – I figured three NY guys would make for good company. Within several minutes of being seated, Joe Pesci walks into the dining room with his friend Carlo. They come over to our table to say hello and Joe asks me if I've seen Lou, who soon showed up. After dining we joined Lou, Joe and Carlo on the terrace for the inevitable cigars. It was a fun night, Frank was pleased to have a great story to tell when he returned to New York, and it enhanced the relationship between our companies.

That time my worlds nicely intersected.

Another, but slightly different example: I was sponsoring a party for a Hells Angel named Rusty Coones at one of their clubhouses. A party to celebrate being removed from federal paper, a welcome-home party of sorts allowing you to freely "associate" with other convicted felons or outlaw biker-club members. It was through other Hells Angel members that I had met Rusty and his wife "KO." Rusty was a giant at 6'7" and 280 pounds (of muscle) and KO sure was a knockout, a beautiful big-hearted woman who also knew how to stand her ground. So when I heard about Rusty's party, I met with then San Fernando Valley Charter President Pete Piccione and gave him some money for the affair, which was also attended by Hells Angels founder Sonny Barger. Present as well were several guys from the charter in Munich. I hung with the Germans for a while since I'd been to Germany many times on business and we struck up a rapport. Fast-forward a year. I'm in Munich for the bi-annual Electronica Trade Show and after being dropped at the hotel by my cabdriver I realize I've forgotten my briefcase in his trunk. By now the driver's long gone. For the next two days I'm trying to retrieve my briefcase with laptop, passport and other important items. To no avail. The night before my flight back I'm in a panic and call Pete Piccione and ask him if his Hells Angel colleagues in Munich might help me out. He'll see what he can do. I'm not very confident so I start investigating the protocol involved in traveling when you've lost your passport. Within an hour of my call to Pete, I get a ring from the cabbie profusely apologizing for not noticing my briefcase in his trunk. Says he'll personally deliver it to my hotel. Twenty minutes later we meet in the lobby, I give him some euros for his trouble, and to this day I don't know what transpired between him and the Munich Hells Angels.

Whatever it was, it proved effective.[6]

The corporate and hoodlum worlds might have intersected but rarely my corporate and familial ones.

I didn't bother sharing my hard-earned business achievement with blood relatives because they cared as much about my success as they did about the price of tea in China.

---

6 In gratitude I later sponsored a couple of their annual Toy Run charitable events. Hey you Munich guys, Johnny lässt grüssen!

With the exception of my closest cousin Iron Mike. We had been writing each other just after he was transferred from the Terre Haute Federal Correction Facility in Indiana to the Federal Correction Facility in Milan, Michigan, where he served most of his term for the FBI weapons-possession charge, and I shared my career news personally with him once he was transferred to the Metropolitan Correction Center in Chicago, which was a halfway house for prisoners whose release dates were approaching and who were slated for re-integration into society. I told him we'd celebrate when he could travel to California and I'd naturally pick up the tab.

Shortly after returning from my visit with Mike, I received one of those bad calls from Chicago. It was the death of another first cousin Larry Jr., son of my father's younger brother Larry Sr. The younger Larry was pretty much a happy-go-lucky kid, good-humored and fun to be around, a bit chubby but when he joined the Air Force he got himself in good shape. Still, he had to take some type of strong medication that resulted in his being medically discharged in his twenties. Larry was only 42 when he died, but it had been a long time coming. Several years earlier he had been involved in a car accident. There were no life-threatening injuries, and from my limited knowledge of the incident it was not his fault. But the family car was damaged and his high-strung father slapped him around at the crash scene. This pushed young Larry over the edge. He told me and Iron Mike about the crash a few days later and said he was going to dedicate the rest of his life to making his father miserable. Knowing he had a screw loose led us to believe his words. A couple years later I learned that he had moved back home with his parents and was living in the basement. I saw him at a wedding and hardly recognized the guy. He must have gained two-hundred pounds – some four-hundred pounds total on a 5'9" frame. It was disturbing.

He was punishing himself to punish his father. His death was most certainly a release.

Things between me and my father had reached an armed truce. He was putting a lot of time and effort into his Pope John Paul II music video, and at his request I invested several thousand dollars for him to re-record a few songs for the video/DVD. A number of us joined him at Capitol Records to watch the recording. Jake was there along with some small-time hoods from Chicago led by a kid we called Jimmy Nails. Just to give you some idea. Also present and overseeing the recording session was Tommy Amato. Tommy was a pro and well known in the entertainment industry, mostly Las Vegas, having been Wayne Newton's first manager and representing my father in Vegas for a short time. Via my father's high-school friend Jerry Coniker we were receiving support from the Catholic Church, and eventually my father would receive a gold-plated cross and medallion created from master-molds that had been given a blessing by JP II at some type of service in the Vatican. I saw letters accompanying the gifts which confirmed their authenticity as well as other letters from cardinals and bishops praising the project.

And then there was the photo of JP II holding a copy of the video.

What could go wrong?

When it came to my father just about everything.

Unbeknownst to me, he was already double-dealing and had collected money from others to re-re-record the very same songs I had already paid for. Should have seen that one coming. His entire life, no matter how great an idea or opportunity, the old man always found a way of sabotaging his success. Always focusing on the short-term score. Whenever I helped him make money on a legit deal he was invariably discontent – I had to convince him that we'd actually *scammed* the money so that he could attain an acceptable level of satisfaction in that twisted mind of his.

Frosting on the cake was his attacking Jerry Coniker with scathing letters and abusive phone calls. I was included in these attacks. All of which were gross misrepresentations.

And suddenly the deal was dead.

But not my rancor. I paid a visit to his office. As for our armed truce, now only the "armed" part applied. I grabbed him and threw him against the wall, my right fist cocked and ready to unload.

"Why are you so violent?"

Yes, he said that. The same man who had constantly forced me into fights – gratuitously, maliciously, for his own sick entertainment. The same man who I'd witnessed attacking man, woman and child. That same man who had beaten my mother to within an inch of her life. I released my grip and turned and walked away leaving a couple guys in the office to figure out what had just happened. My father certainly wouldn't tell them. Not the truth at least.

That was the last time I ever saw him.

But I would have one final opportunity to beat him at his own game.

I like calling this one the "triple-cross."

As we shared the exact same name, my father periodically used my social-security number if any money came in since it would otherwise be subject to garnishment in order to satisfy his judge-ordered restitution of the "marks" he had victimized – and restitution to the tune of 170K. My father could be kept on probation as long as he owed that money. This enabled the authorities to keep a close eye on him. And boy did they ever. I'd heard on more than one occasion that the Florida judiciary had it out for gangsters from Chicago and New York pulling hustles in their state. The terms of my father's probation included submitting monthly reports on his activities as well as monthly income statements under penalty of perjury – and that's why he was making free with my social-security number.

At this time he had somehow gained possession of a vacant building in Chicago. Some crackheads were squatting there and local law enforcement was attempting to contact the owner of the building in order to report damage to a couple windows. Apparently they couldn't reach my father – which made sense, as he'd been picked up on a parole violation and extradited to the Broward County Correctional facility in Florida. But in using my social-security number my father had made the mistake of also listing my company as his place of employment. And my company was where I took the call from the reporting officer for the broken windows. He told me the situation and when I heard him say "your building" I knew that my father was somehow involved.

I said: "Could you please verify the exact address so we know we're talking about the same building."

He gave it to me.

"That's it all right," I said. "Don't worry, I'll handle the damages."

"Thank you, sir, and thank you for your time."

I hung up and then punched in my father's number. But his cell phone went directly to voicemail. I made calls to a couple relatives but they had no idea where he was either. Finally it occurred to me that he may have been picked up for some petty bullshit and given a short stint, this being the pattern with him and his parole officer as well as the Florida DA – both of whom hated him. So I contacted attorney Andy Yurcho, a friend of mine who had agreed to represent my father as a favor to me, and he said that Mario had been picked up and was back in jail and it would be at least a month before his hearing date because of a major backup in the Broward County system.

My Sicilian revenge-gene was activated.

I called a couple business friends to find both a good Chicago lawyer and a local real-estate agent. After telephone consultations I took a red eye from LAX to O'Hare, keeping my arrival secret from family members for obvious reasons. It was through the realtor that I learned of a couple liens and a second mortgage on the property but nothing the equity couldn't cover. Then I had the damage fixed, put the building up for sale and flew back to LA – but not before telling the realtor that I valued my privacy and he should guard my personal information in the event of inquiries.

I was astonished at how easily this property sold. Within a week I had two offers and countered both and then closed in thirty days. Six weeks later the realtor called me and said he'd received several distressed calls from people alleging to be family members and wanting to know who sold the property. One call was from an attorney claiming to represent me. I asked the attorney's name and then did some research and found there was no record of him having ever been a member of the Illinois bar.

My father, who prided himself on his street-savvy ways, had inadvertently set himself up for me to take this property right out from under his nose! And the funny thing is I finally understood the thrill he experienced in pulling this kind of caper. I was far more excited about beating him at his own game than I was with gaining any financial payback – though I did restitute a couple of my friends whom my father had conned, and when the smoke cleared I had in fact recovered all the money he'd robbed from me over the years – and at a substantial rate of return.

After any particular score, including when he would take

me for money, my father would put a big grin on his face and ask: "Did you learn anything?" Or alternately: "Who was that masked man?" But these weren't real questions so much as rhetorical victory laps in smug celebration of his superior street smarts. Now I was sorely tempted to give him a phone call and throw one of those lines back in his teeth. But I knew that complete denial of any involvement would make him crazier than just stuffing it down his throat. For months I received calls from family members asking if I was behind the sale of the building. I knew they were calling on my father's behalf and I never let on – it was driving him batshit!

On the legit work front, Jimmy P had asked that I set up a meeting with one of our largest medical customers located in Minnesota. I did and he and I agreed to hook up in Chicago for drinks with my brother Bill and Iron Mike before flying out to Minneapolis. A few nights before the trip I was expected at the Rendezvous Bar for my monthly Boxing Program Fundraiser. The Rendezvous was only a block from the community center. This was one of my hangouts (the same place where Iron Mike had punched out that cockstrong moron some years back) so the staff and owners let me conduct my fundraisers here. The patrons were a rougher crowd and always supportive of the program by bidding on the boxing program's T-shirts and tank-tops that I brought to auction off.

Since I was preoccupied with the Minnesota trip, I'd forgotten about the fundraiser until I received a call from one of my fighters whom I was supposed to meet at the bar. I threw a leather jacket over my Dago Tee, pulled on a pair of heavy boots, and headed to the Rendezvous. After selling the shirts, I bellied up to the bar with my fighter, a professional featherweight named Juan Ruiz. We were talking shop when a tall skinny drunk came over and stood close enough to infringe my personal space and told me to move over. He was obviously looking for trouble because there was no one within ten feet of us. I took a deep breath and told him take it easy and we'd slide down to give him whatever room he needed. Apparently we weren't fast enough for him because he gave me a push on the shoulder. I responded by staying put and not deigning him a glance. A shift in tactics. If only for a change. If only for the sake of experimentation. Grow and develop. The old self's getting boring. But out of the corner of my eye I saw him now turned toward me with his chest puffed out and in decent range for a short right cross...

"So like I say," I addressed Juan. "You wanna stay out of street fights cuz you'll fuck up your hands –"

WHAM!

My punch landed high on his cheekbone. Problem was he was too close and I was unable to pop my elbow high enough to catch him on the chin. And my timing was off, possibly because I was wearing biker boots which are hard to pivot off and thereby putting my upper and lower body out of sync. On his way down he was able to grab the lapel of my jacket and I landed on top of him, my knees on either side of his skinny frame, trying to punch his face, his arms crossed to deflect my blows, my leather jacket restricting me from throwing wider punches, and then the sole doorman jumping in and lifting me off this troublemaker. As I was lifted I felt pain in my ankle and couldn't put any weight on it. While they were throwing the other guy out I stood supporting myself on the bar and the barmaid bought me a shot of whiskey and asked if I was okay. I told her I thought I might have sprained my ankle but was otherwise fine. I downed the shot then told Juan I was going home to ice my ankle.

"Oh yeah," I added, "and stay out of bar fights too."

I really had been telling Juan to keep cool on the street so that his hands would be in good shape for the ring. That had been our exact conversation when the drunken idiot came along. That's why I'd been so amenable at first. Practice what you preach. Though admittedly I'd never been much good at that.

When I got home I took off my boots. My left ankle wasn't swollen but there was a small discolored bump. I kept it elevated and iced it for an hour and went to bed. When I awoke the next morning I was still unable to put weight on it so I went to get an X-ray and discovered I had a clean break and would need a walking cast.

Seventeen

Did You Learn Anything?

I gave Jimmy a call and came clean regarding my latest altercation.

"How on earth do you break your ankle in a bar fight?"

"I'm asking myself the same question."

"I'll see you in Chicago."

I knew Jimmy would understand but still break my balls relentlessly throughout our business trip – which he did. In Chicago we had a great time hanging out with my brother and cousin Iron Mike at Rocky's, the very same bar where we held Mike's going-away party a couple years earlier. My extended cousin Anthony Palermo had attended that affair and now I learned that the revolving door was in full swing because he was about to serve a four-year sentence for obstruction of justice. Jimmy P was as comfortable with my family as he was with his ultra-rich peer group – and the servers at the bar loved him because while remaining a regular guy he sure didn't tip like one.

The next day we boarded our short flight to Minneapolis for the high-level meeting with a large medical-device manufacturer. Upon entering the meeting room on crutches and greeting our executive counterparts I was immediately asked what happened.

"I didn't meet my quarterly sales number for this account," I said. "This is a tough company."

That got a laugh, helping to loosen the mood, and after ironing out a few major issues the meeting resulted in a nice $36 million order. But I won't take credit for that. I was soon to learn that everything Jimmy touched turned to gold.

Our stock was rising and things with Janell had reached the point that a few months later at an Executive Managers meeting in Cancun Mexico – to which spouses and significant others were invited – I asked her to marry me. It was at dinner this night with the other executives and their partners that I announced our engagement and we all celebrated. Jimmy P would be my Best Man at the wedding in Jamaica. The choice of Jamaica was largely what I call an "un-invite" – though sending formal invitations to a number of relatives, I knew they wouldn't be flying to Jamaica. A tip to avoid unwanted kin: marry offshore.

After just a year of marriage Janell became pregnant – with twins no less. I guess when you start so late in the game, having multiples was just making up for lost time. Then my second set of twins was born. This was truly a freak of nature – my wife dropped eggs like I dropped F-bombs. The company was growing at an equally rapid pace. I had my hands full and there was no room for any monkey business. On weekends and after work I spent my time at home with my family. Although occasionally I would venture out. One day I received a call from Johnny Fratto, asking me to meet him for dinner at The Rainbow, that restaurant on Sunset Boulevard where I was introduced to Hugh Hefner. This was a strange call because Johnny seldom left the confines of his Beverly Hills condo.

We sat at a booth and ordered roasted peppers to start. As we're waiting Johnny's gaze drifts over to this couple that ends up sitting in the booth next to ours. They're well dressed; both seem to be in their late fifties. As they're being seated Johnny turns his head and looks to be having a pleasant conversation with the guy – when suddenly Johnny leaps up and leans over into the other booth and takes a swipe at the guy – not a punch but a kind of slap designed not so much to hurt as completely emasculate another man. But then Johnny thinks better of it and proceeds to land a couple closed-fist punches. I jump up and grab him by the back of his drawers and set him down. The guy in the booth is completely stunned. The woman has that deer-in–the-headlights look. I see the manager observing the incident, so I catch his eye and shake my head, the last thing we need is cops. But I can't figure it out. Because then Johnny starts talking to me about something completely unrelated. As if nothing has happened. Our roasted peppers come and then our steaks and the whole time I'm looking over Johnny's shoulder at the guy he just worked over to make certain he doesn't grow balls and take a cheap shot at Johnny. But little chance of that. When not holding his head in his hands he wipes his forehead with a handkerchief. The woman is gazing off into space. They say nothing the entire time. Their food comes and they just stare at it. Not eating a bite. But also not leaving. Or even switching booths. Like they're chained there. We finish our steaks. As we rise to go Johnny mumbles something I can't hear to the frozen couple and then moves off. I stay standing and tell the guy: "Whatever problem you have with Johnny, you should settle it quickly." I turn to the woman: "I'm sure that Johnny extends his apologies for ruining your dinner."

I feel like an actor in a walk-on role for a play whose plot has been kept secret from him.

I catch up with Johnny. "So what was all that back there?"

"The guy stole a jacket from my daughter. Fucking

expensive. Some 10K."

"You pick a great place to set him straight."

"Seize the moment."

"Like I did twenty-five years ago in the Viking restaurant – you remember that – where I did a number on the boyfriend of my half-sister?"

"Sure, I remember."

"And you remember what you said?"

"Tell me."

"That I had to control myself in public places."

"So I took lessons from you."

It was about this time that I received word through mutual friends that Jake had been indicted on a money-laundering charge stemming from the arrest of a kid they'd caught speeding through Texas carrying over 150K in cash two years earlier. When I finally talked to Jake he said he would plead the Fifth before a grand jury and if he had to do time then he would do time. I didn't dwell on it because Jake had always been solid. But even if he folded to law-enforcement pressure and cut a deal to name names, pulling a Henry Hill to lessen his jail time, this was a white-collar crime that had little to do with the blue-collar world of hoodlums and bikers we both frequented. My friends, I thought, were rat-proof. So I dismissed the thing from my mind. I just figured the revolving door was in play again. Nothing new here.

My company was growing rapidly, and with each new acquisition came redundancy and conflicts of interest which needed to be remedied. In other words this eternal state of flux was wreaking havoc with our sales organization, and since we had become a global player it necessitated international travel on my part to update and adjust to changes made a year earlier. Granted I wasn't the most cosmopolitan of guys. I'd been to Europe once or twice but at that time didn't know

Slovenia from Slovakia or Liechtenstein from Frankenstein and frankly didn't care. The executives were a bit concerned about my rough edges. Jimmy's last words prior to my first Europe trip were: "Please Johnny, no international incidents, I don't want to read about you in the news!" That would have been nice – to have even had *time* to cause an international incident. I flew to Ireland for a business dinner that same evening, the next morning took a flight to Charleroi, Belgium, for a two-hour meeting and lunch with company executives, then boarded a slow-moving train to Brussels to catch the high-speed rail to Paris for a dinner engagement and meetings all the next day, this followed by a morning flight to Milan for two meetings and back to the U.S. the subsequent morning.

Other trips were just as frenetic. I won't bore you with all the business minutiae, but to give you the flavor here are some condensed journal excerpts from three junkets I undertook to very contrasting parts of the world:

East Asia. I fly out of LAX to Hong Kong and then head to Macau on the ferry where I learn that the American notion of personal space no longer applies. The people are uncomfortably close and even rubbing up against you from all sides. While exiting the ferry it feels like some joker has his fingers in my belt loop and I turn on him: "If you get any closer you better have a fucking engagement ring for me." It's unlikely he understands the words but my body language is unmistakable and he moves a safe distance away. I can't bark at people all day and night, though, so I just have to adjust to this culture of crowding. The ferry lands us right in front of the casinos, I grab a cab to the hotel where I have just enough time to check into my room, splash water on my face, and head to one of the ballrooms where some hundred local employees along with new reps and distributors listen to me explain the latest acquisition and shake-up in our Asian sales force. This followed by lunch with key Asian representatives, some afternoon technical training on new products, then dinner with direct employees to provide additional details on the structural changes and my expectations of their performance on a quarter-by-quarter basis; we drink several shots of what is referred to as Chinese White Wine but which can only be described as a combination of Italian grappa and diesel fuel. Next morning back on the ferry to Hong Kong and then a flight to Tokyo where I go from Narita Airport straight to a meeting with a new Japanese manufacturer's rep I'm considering hiring to cover specific customers in Japan. At the proposed client's office in Shinjuku I also meet with his CEO and tour their offices, and that evening we rendezvous again for a traditional Japanese dinner. These dinners are long and entail multiple courses of food that I generally don't recognize, and sitting on the floor with no support is not great for my recent lower-back pain. Which at least prevents me from falling asleep. After enduring this event we go to the Shinjuku Park Hyatt for a nightcap. My hotel is walking distance from the restaurant, very swanky and has a great bar on the 52nd floor where – my counterparts are proud to inform me – they shot the movie *Lost in Translation* starring Bill Murray. After a couple snifters of Anisette I call it a night and thank them for their hospitality and next morning it's back to L.A.

Russia. The connecting flight is from Frankfurt. My colleague and I are unaware that Lufthansa affords shuttle service to first-class passengers, so we go through the same checkpoint two or three times before finding our gate. In arriving at Domodedovo Airport in Moscow we're greeted by a driver who takes us to a hotel near Red Square where I rest briefly before having dinner at an Italian restaurant with representatives from an international law firm to discuss a particular issue concerning ITAR (International Trade and Arms Regulations). The next day a talk before Russian aerospace engineers, and I don't start speaking until all their headsets are in place for the simultaneous translation. In scanning their ranks I can see they are hardened people – all older men who sit stone-faced throughout my presentation. After the forum ends several hours later we hold a number of face-to-face meetings with the interpreting done by our Russian sales representatives, who afterward take us to Red Square via the Moscow subway. This is an experience in itself. People always talk about how beautiful the Moscow subway is but they never tell you about the beggars at the top of every escalator. Adults in dirty tattered clothing accompanied by children with grotesquely disfigured faces and mangled limbs. Tough to look at. They remind me of those kids at the Crippled Children's Society some four decades back. These vagrants make the U.S. homeless look like full-fledged members of the solid middle class. Red Square is lit up nicely and we take pictures in front of Lenin's Tomb. Next day at the Domodedovo Airport I notice damage at the entrance to the terminal, where construction crews are working, and which I'm told is the result of a Chechen suicide bomber who killed 37 people. Back in Frankfurt we've learned our lesson and jump directly onto the shuttle waiting on the tarmac.

India. Longest flight I've ever experienced. Sixteen hours from LAX to Dubai and a four-hour connecting flight to Bangalore where I jump in a cab and head to the Leela Palace – my hotel. A guard with a machine gun stands watch as I go through a metal detector just outside the entryway. The Leela Palace has lush scenic grounds replete with waterfalls. I take a peek at the ballroom where our all-day forum will be taking place tomorrow. Big and opulent and with video screens halfway down the room on either side for those far from the stage, which I'm pleased to see is also large, as I prefer walking around when making my presentation. Along with representatives from various private entities, my audience the next day is mainly design and components engineers from the Indian Space and Research Organization, which is essentially the government space agency. My talk goes off without a glitch. Next day we pack up and head to the airport for a short flight to Ahmedabad and this time staying at the Sheraton. The drive from the airport is an obstacle course, the streets buzzing with motor scooters, bicycles and other diminutive vehicles; random goats, dogs and cows roaming the streets among the vehicles; not a single traffic light or stop sign but just here and there a guy in uniform attempting to direct traffic but being completely ignored. The highlight: a scooter ridden by a family of four laden with household items and weaving in and out of all this madness. At the Sheraton more guards with machine guns who walk a German shepherd (presumably a bomb-sniffing dog) around our cab while also checking under it with one of those long-handled mirrors, and then another metal detector prior to entering the hotel. I'm told that the security is heightened in wake of a recent terrorist attack in Mumbai. After freshening up in my room I come down to the lobby where I meet our country manager (his name Parag) who has arranged transportation to our conference, which is not at the Sheraton but some other hotel. The transportation is an old bus with what looks like Arabic markings on the side and odd hanging decor inside each window. I say: "No fucking chance I get into that Al Qaeda death bus!" After prodding by colleagues I board with great caution and hesitancy. The forum is in a large basement below the hotel lobby and which I am told is the best spot because it remains cooler here than any other conference room. I blast through my opening remarks and corporate overview (the same one I gave in Moscow) and have time for a few questions from the audience. One guy asks about the average size of the computer hard-drive in an average UAV (unmanned aerial vehicle). I say it depends on the mission but that non-classified information regarding a specific model of UAV would indicate somewhere between 300 to 400 gigabytes – and when I ask if this answers his question he gives an odd bobble of his head. I ask again and he gives me the same bobble-head motion. I ask a third time. Now he bobbles and squirms both. I see some of my better-versed colleagues in Indian culture signaling me to back off and later they inform me that the bobble-head response is equivalent to saying "I understand." The day wears on, a couple power outages, the cool basement turns hot, then it's back to the death bus for the return ride to the hotel. Only it won't start. Parag gathers strangers off the street to help push the bus away from the hotel and make room for the replacement bus he has waiting down the road, just a minute or two distant, but he won't allow us to walk. Death bus or no, I'm putting in a good word for this guy with his superiors . . .

It was during this period that I received another one of those Chicago phone calls. My father had died of a massive heart attack. I flew to Chicago for the funeral, leaving my wife and kids safely ensconced at home. At the funeral parlor I learned my father was broke, so my inheritance was one-third of his funeral expenses. As I looked down at his open casket one of his pet phrases occurred to me: "The meek shall inherit the earth – six feet of it!" Meek or no, it's your turn now, pops. At the wake I did my best to avoid most of my family members with the exception of a couple cousins and my brother Bill. At one point he and I were alone and started talking and he said:

"You know Dad never did get over that triple cross you pulled."

"Who told him it was me?"

"No one. He figured it out for himself. Who else could it have been?"

"Any number of guys who had it in for him."

"The funny thing is, I think he enjoyed the idea of you having done it. Like only a son of his could have pulled a caper like that."

"Had I known I would have told him I had nothing to do with it."

"Almost like he was proud of you."

"It would have been the first time. Nothing I ever accomplished rated his approval before."

"Well, this sure did," said Bill. "Every time your name came up in conversation he'd shake his head and say he'd have done the same thing had the opportunity arisen. It sounds twisted but I think that was probably his highest compliment. That you'd outscammed the scammer. By the way, you're a pallbearer."

Why not? I was a good pallbearer, had gotten lots of practice over the years.

The next morning we all sat in church openly laughing as the priest performing the eulogy gave humorous account of how he too had been taken for money by my father. The trusting priest had been severely reprimanded by church leaders. Not your typical eulogy. Later at the lunch reception the priest came to my table and asked to speak with me privately. I obliged and we distanced ourselves from the table.

"John, do you intend to follow through on that promise to honor your father's pledge?"

"What pledge?"

"The thirty-thousand dollars he pledged to the church."

"What's that got to do with me?"

He explained that after my father had taken him for a ride

he got a pang of conscience and promised the church eventual reparations but knew his health was poor and that's where I came in.

"Your father assured me that if anything happened to him then his rich son in California would honor the pledge. He said you two had spoken. He said that you'd be good for the thirty-thousand come what may."

I had to disappoint him. But it was a fitting conclusion to my father's life, pulling a post-mortem con job like that and getting in one last jab at me. I felt like asking the priest if he'd learned anything, but sensed he was a slow learner.

EIGHTEEN

A Made Man

It wasn't long after my father's death that I came up on the half-century mark and Janell threw me a 50th birthday bash.

She'd done this kind of thing in the past. Like my fortieth birthday at the Amazon Restaurant and for drinks afterward at the Barfly on Sunset. That was the first time my worlds collided on a grand scale. Bikers, mobsters and boxers coming up against actors, businessmen and other more genteel sorts. I would personally have preferred to keep these worlds separate but had no say regarding the guest-list since it had been a surprise party. I guess the highlight was when two Vagos bikers, under orders from Terry "The Tramp" Orrendorf, escorted me to the men's room at Barfly and made everyone exit, including one of my corporate friends and the attendant handing out paper towels and mints, who himself was instructed to keep others out until we were done. Try pissing in comfort while two gigantic outlaw bikers stand guard on either side of your urinal.

"A bit much don't you think guys?"

"The Tramp said to make sure you had a good time with no problems."

I hoped that'd be the case this time around for my 50th.

We had security at the door and I'd even considered a metal detector – but finally decided against it since I didn't want to alarm my guests. Ten years on, the genteel crowd had grown in number. Not only actors and company executives but bestselling authors, high-profile lawyers, doctors and politicians as well as local news and radio personalities. A couple Playboy playmates thrown into the mix. Several high-school and college friends. But the non-genteel side of the equation – the assorted thugs and criminals – hadn't grown any less. Despite all those who'd landed in jail or ended up dead in the intervening decade. There were some days when I'd wake up more than mildly surprised that I wasn't among their number.

Our 100-foot long pool had temporary scaffolding in its middle supporting a dance floor painted with JOHNNY'S 50TH in big block letters. DJ Crash, who did a lot of Hugh Hefner's parties, was stationed mid-pool behind the elevated jacuzzi and squarely above the bronze lion's head affixed to the jacuzzi's wall, which usually had a waterfall streaming down it but which we'd of course turned off for the event. There was enough liquid flowing that evening – plenty of booze as well as Italian food catered by my restaurateur friend Johnny Nardone, and after the feasting my wife made her way to the microphone. Okay, they have to sing Happy Birthday, let's get that out of the way. Instead she announced that there would be a series of speakers and then introduced Scott Baio who came to the mic and beckoned me to take a seat in a chair he placed next to the microphone. Oh shit, I thought, how about that nice round of Happy Birthday! I took my seat and as expected Scott tore into me – in the nicest possible way of course – skewering me through a comic recounting of my life's more memorable episodes. After Scott's monologue he acted as MC by introducing one speaker after the next, DJ Crash playing personalized music for each as they approached the mic, and it turned into an hour of unmitigated ball-breaking.

Mainly because there was so much material to work with.

After this lambasting I sat back down with my drink. Earlier in the evening I had been going from table to table, greeting and joking with my guests, but now I was content to just sit back and take it all in. And in so doing I felt something missing. Something within me. Something that had long been there but was now strangely absent.

My abiding hatred.

That hatred which had accompanied me all my adult life and much of my youth had dissipated if not completely vanished – the same hatred which had driven me to succeed, leave my mark, show my family and the world I wouldn't be beat – a hatred that didn't so much turn lemons into lemonade as poison the damn lemonade and serve it back to those I resented. If only by proxy. And prime target of that resentment being my father. But whose bequest of hatred had been finally laid to rest.

What had done it?

Not his death but life. The life I now saw all around me. My four children, my wife Janell, my friends and associates and other fine companions on this journey through human existence. But the human heart, like nature, abhors a vacuum and a new sentiment had come to replace the hatred. Namely gratitude. A gratitude owing both to the happiness I'd lately experienced and the fact that through all my trials I had somehow retained my faith in God and a very real love of country which now gracefully dovetailed with my career. Whenever feeling sorry for myself in the past it was memory of The Crippled Children's Society which had served as negative corrective: Maybe I had it bad but nowhere near as bad as those kids. This now largely replaced though by a positive feeling of gratitude for not only my loved ones but an extraordinarily game CEO who lets you write your own job description allowing entry to of all things the world of government relations. Interacting with senators, congressmen and the U.S. State Department on issues of national-security technology is stressful but nonetheless a privilege. You can also appreciate things that many take for granted when invited as a Distinguished Visitor onto aircraft carriers and given a first-hand taste of catapult takeoffs and tail-hook landings by brave men and women who protect our freedoms and whose fortunes rise and fall with the quality of your product. And you can gain particular perspective when you realize that all your past dealings with drug traffickers, bookies, bikers, con men and gangsters perfectly prepares you for contracting with Washington politicians, bureaucrats, cyber-security experts and NSA officials.

Joking of course!

Or am I.

But let's just say an easy transition. Because that had been my life - negotiating on the corner of Main and Mean Street. I was leaving that corner now, though, for a leisurely stroll down Main. And never looking back. Just keeping my eyes fixed on the road ahead and maybe even walking the straight and narrow.

EPILOGUE

Juan Azcarate – In 1984, Juan was run over by a drunk driver while checking the engine of a stalled car on the shoulder of the 405 Freeway in Los Angeles. The drunk driver broke Juan's knee, femur, pelvis, clavicle, two ribs, and ruptured his spleen. Juan ended up under the drunk driver's car with battery acid, hot radiator fluid and oil pouring over his right side and leaving third-degree burns on his face, arms and chest. Juan miraculously survived after months in the hospital and dozens of surgeries. Juan is now a home-mortgage consultant and volunteer at the Grossman Burn Center, helping others get through their burn injuries, and he also gives public talks for MADD (Mothers Against Drunk Driving).

John "Sinbad" Baima (stepbrother) – now an executive at a private aerospace company in Wichita, Kansas, where he lives with his wife Robyn. His four boys are grown and pursuing their own careers in Austin, Texas.

Scott Baio – is retired and spends time with his family. His favorite pastimes are playing golf and smoking cigars.

Bill (brother) – a police detective in a suburb outside Chicago.

Ralph Brandi – is retired and an avid fisherman and hunter.

Margie Brockert (sister) – successfully reentered society in 2000 and was released from parole in 2004. She now works with her three grown sons in the vitamin-supplement business.

Jacob "Jake" Cancelli – In an effort to avoid prison time for a pump-and-dump stock scheme, Jake entered the Witness Protection Program and became a confidential informant for the Department of Homeland Security. He testified in a murder trial stemming from a confrontation between the Hells Angels and Vagos motorcycle clubs at a casino in Sparks, Nevada. It is rumored that Jake has testified in other trials under other aliases and he may have been wearing a wire at my 50th birthday party.

Eddie "Cruiser" Caruso – passed away in April 2002 at age 69 from heart disease. Eddie spent a few months with me in California shortly before he died. I had far more meaningful conversations with Eddie than I ever had with my father.

Tony Centracchio – died in 2001 at age 71 while awaiting trial on federal racketeering charges.

Rusty Coones – still a Hells Angel and has become successful in the entertainment world playing the character "Quinn" in the popular FX series "Sons of Anarchy." Rusty recently completed his first screenplay. He lives in Orange County with his charming wife KO.

Carol Costello (stepmother) – don't know and don't care.

John Costello (younger half-brother) – teaches physics at Lincoln Tech in Illinois.

Larry Costello (paternal uncle) – fell asleep while smoking in November 2015 and died in the resultant fire at age 74. Larry was a consummate teaser and generally fun to be around, but like my other relatives, I held a deep-seated resentment toward him because I knew he was aware that his brother has nearly beaten my mother to death, knew of the other family and their vastly better living conditions than ours, and yet not a compassionate word was ever spoken to me acknowledging my mother's fate. Consequently, I considered my uncle as more of an acquaintance than family.

Tommy Costello (paternal uncle) – retired and living in Chicago; same relationship as above.

Steve Cuccio – happily married and living in Las Vegas; a consultant in the entertainment field.

Arlene Damofle (fraternal aunt) – still lives in the same north side home where I lived several summers sharing the basement room of my cousin and closest relative Iron Mike. Arlene is also my godmother and always made me feel welcome.

Frank D'Angelo (aka "Sonny D") – Sonny's explosive temper was on full display in the courtroom when he threw a chair at a federal judge - and luckily missed. He was still charged with assault, and after being forced to take a "vacation," Sonny made his way to Los Angeles to try and make it in the film business. Seems fitting that he ended up doing stunt work and eventually became a stunt coordinator. He is now semi-retired and lives in Las Vegas, going to L.A. on occasion to work as a technical advisor on various TV shows.

Bart Devaney – successful entrepreneur living in San Luis Obispo, California.

Georgia Durante – authored the book *The Company She Keeps: The Dangerous Life of a Model Turned Mafia Wife,* and a kindred spirit in that she always had a foot in two opposing worlds, though eventually distancing herself from the mob and speaking in prisons and women's shelters to help inspire thousands of women to make better choices in life. After retiring from the stunt-driving world due to a stunt gone wrong, she adopted a baby and now rents her home ("The Enchanted Manor") for weddings and location-filming. It's a cliché but it has to be said: she's a woman who constantly reinvents herself.

Mike Ecklund (aka "Iron Mike") – for unknown reasons, in March 2013, my cousin Mike took his own life with a gunshot to the head. Mike was by far my closest relative.

Dominic Ferrara – no longer a Hells Angel and whereabouts unknown.

Miguel Flores - recently retired from patrolling the streets of Chicago: but you can see him playing his beloved harmonica on YouTube at "Chicago's Cop jamming @ Do Division Street Fest!"

Johnny Fratto Sr. – Johnny went to the doctor in 2015 for a cough, only to find he had stage-four cancer, dying in November of that year.

Carolina Gallentine (half-sister) – no longer on the talk-show circuit; now a sales executive at a private medical firm.

Father Leo Glueckert O. Carm. – writes articles, delivers lectures, and is involved in alumni affairs. He is author of *Desert Springs in the City: A Concise History of the Carmelites*. Father Leo baptized all four of my children.

Dino Guglielmelli – is serving a ten-year sentence for solicitation of murder of his estranged wife (detailed on the television series "48 Hours" and its episode "The Millionaire, the Model & the Hitman"). Based on my experiences the entire case was a sham – the wife and alleged "hitman" are liars of the worst sort.

Hugh Hefner – died in September of 2017 from cardiac arrest.

Louis Ippolito (aka "Lou Ipps") – was imprisoned for thirteen years on the charge of marijuana possession with intent to sell, which today is legal in most states. Lou now lives in Florida with his girlfriend Elena Garcia in a beautiful townhouse; they also have a second home in Italy. He paints in oils and does a little writing to keep himself busy, and of course still loves his cigars. He has never been so content, even more so than when he was a millionaire, and Lou would have it known that "money does not bring happiness, it's love and companionship."

Father John Knoernschild O. Carm. – not long after baptizing my first set of twins in a joint ceremony with Father Leo, he became director of the National Shrine of Saint Therese in Darien, Illinois. Father John died 14 November 2010 in Naperville, Illinois, at age 66 of brain cancer.

Kevin McAleer – received his PhD in modern European history from the University of California and now lives as a writer and translator in Berlin.

Lori Mele (paternal half-sister) – living in Vermont with her three beautiful children.

Father Don Merrifield SJM – served as President of Loyola Marymount University from 1969 to 1984 and died in February 2010 of a heart attack at 81 years old. I regret not having properly thanked Father Merrifield for his help at LMU.

Christopher "Pipes" Metropoulos – left the Chicago Outlaws MC and his whereabouts are unknown.

Terry "The Tramp" Orrendorf – was no longer active in the Vagos MC, when he passed away from heart failure in April of 2018 in Southern California. Orrendorf is the subject of *Terry the Tramp: The Life and Dangerous Times of a One Percenter*, where he declares himself the best leader that the Vagos MC has ever had or will have.

Linda "The Merry Widow" Pacino (fraternal aunt) – after the shooting death of her first husband Paul in 1974 and the deaths of her next two husbands under unusual circumstances, Linda has since found it difficult to get dates. I will never forget the August night in 1974 when she explained to us in great detail the controversial killing of my uncle Paul. Not your typical family conversation.

Anthony Palermo – after serving four years in prison, Tony rebounded and is back selling cars and flipping houses. Tony lives outside of Chicago and periodically visits me when he comes to Los Angeles. His record remains unblemished at 100-0 in street fights.

James Peterson (aka "Jimmy P") – was promoted from CEO to CEO and Chairman of the Board in November of 2013. Under his leadership the company has grown from $250 million to $6 billion in market cap. Jimmy P is godfather to my firstborn.

Pete Piccione – I briefly spoke to Pete at Johnny Fratto's funeral but have no idea what he is doing now. Since he was patched up, I assume he is still with the Hells Angels.

James Reiss – decades after starting a very successful law firm, Jim pleaded no contest to two felony counts of grand theft and was recently released after serving nearly half of a ten-year sentence. He is now dedicated to rebuilding his business.

Mark Richardson – a transition took place in his life with a missionary trip to Uganda in 2008. Now he is very involved in his church, working in Men's Ministry, and otherwise lives a calm and quiet life on a small ranch with his wife and two grown children and a grandson.

Dr. Mark Saginor – practices medicine in Century City, California, and remains my personal physician, close friend and confidant.

Frank Stalzer – after living in New York for 54 years, Frank and his wife Maria decided to relocate to a quieter part of the country and now reside in Charlottesville, Virginia, on a five-acre estate in the picturesque Blue Ridge Mountains. Frank is currently the owner of VEC Supply, a distributor of data communications and security products. Frank and I still keep in touch on a regular basis.

Jimmy Van Patten – spokesperson for Dick Van Patten's Natural Balance Pet Foods. Just finished co-starring with Nicolas Cage and Gina Gershon in the motion picture *Inconceivable* and will be producing and starring with his brother Vincent Van Patten in the feature film *Walk to Vegas*, which is scheduled to shoot in April 2017. He remains very close to his mom and brothers and he continues to pursue the dream and lifestyle that his father Dick Van Patten embodied and always wanted for his own children.

John Visciglia – lifelong and only friend that knew my mother, lives in Newport Beach, California. Married nine years with two step-daughters and two granddaughters. Presently working as a counselor treating substance abuse and as a Division 1 college- baseball umpire in the Big West Conference and Western Athletic Conference.

Christopher Walsh – it was on 2 July 2003 that Chris' remains were discovered concealed in a container in a public-storage unit in Van Nuys, California. An autopsy revealed that Walsh had been shot to death. The murder remained a mystery for years until Chris' brother Dennis Walsh wrote a book called *Nobody Walks: Bringing My Brother's Killers to Justice*, which helped in solving the murder.

AFTERWORD

I met Johnny at a party. I thought he was insane. He claimed to be an aerospace and defense sub-contractor executive, and yet he spoke like Tony Soprano. He looked and dressed corporate but based on his upbringing in the streets of Chicago, one would've thought he'd wind up as a cop, priest or "outfit" guy, like his father.

How does a Chicago street hood end up as a family man with two sets of twins, who goes off to work carrying a briefcase, drives a Maserati, and sits down for lunch with a United States Senator to initialize a national-security infrastructure plan?

What?!?

Johnny told me about his upbringing in Chicago, his dashing singer -mobster father -and I couldn't wait to get away from him. This man has seen way too many *Godfather* movies, I thought. Nobody's life is that dramatic. Who faces death at the hands of Chicago mobsters because of a scheme conceived by his father to scam the mobsters?

Well, the same people invited me to the same party the next year, and I saw Johnny again. This time, he volunteered that his mom died when he was young, her death most likely the result of a savage beating at the hands of his father.

I had my own difficulties with my former Marine father, who I thought unnecessarily gruff and harsh. But unnecessarily harsh versus a father who beat your mother so savagely that he nearly killed her? That's pretty intense. How do you overcome that? How do you live without bitterness and anger? I still thought this was fiction.

The following year, I saw Johnny again at the party. This time, I asked more questions. What kind of relationship did you have with your father after your mom died? Do you have siblings? How are they affected? How did you end up being an executive with a prestigious publicly traded technology company, given that your dad must have wanted you to follow in his footsteps?

Then he also told me about his father's singing voice, every bit the gift possessed by Sinatra, Como and Damone.

And speaking of Vic Damone, the story about how Johnny's father out-sang Vic Damone at Chicago's annual Italian Fest is worth the price of admission. As for Johnny, he was forced to pull money-stealing capers as a kid, boxed as an amateur, was a High School All-American in track, ran with Chicago ruffians then went to college - the first and only in his family to do so, and where he became the captain of the rowing team. Captain of his rowing team?

By now, I was fascinated by Johnny's life. "Have you thought about writing a book?" I asked. He said no, not thinking his life particularly interesting, and he wasn't a writer. "Are you kidding?" I said. "Your life is a walking *Goodfellas* movie, only far more interesting." I told him the book should be in his voice, but with structure. The more we talked, the more he realized how unique his life has been - and how people could benefit from how he overcame.

To prepare for the book, Johnny and I met with more than thirty friends, relatives and associates. We listened to Johnny Sr.'s music catalogue, searched newspaper articles and archives, and watched television news broadcasts about the Big Scam that threatened to get Johnny Sr. and his son killed.

We are products of the relationships we had with our mothers and fathers whether for ill or for good, whether you had a good father or a bad one. And Johnny's story is one of survival and triumph despite- and yet because of - his father.

Frankly, I think writing *Executive Hoodlum* was cathartic for him – and a lot cheaper than therapy.

Larry Elder

Acknowledgments

There are people and institutions that kept me somewhat balanced during the unrelenting chaos surrounding my family life. During each stage of my personal evolution those mentioned below likely had no idea how much I appreciated their friendship and support. Their impact is incalculable.

The Catholic schools I attended helped reinforce some type of moral base. Carmelites Father Leo Glueckert, Father Tom Batsis, the late Father John Knoernschild and Jesuit Father Don Merrifield kept me somewhat balanced during the high-school and college years, maintaining my faith in God and humanity.

I absorbed small doses of logic and sanity over the decades from old friends Juan Azcarate, Kevin McAleer, Bart Devaney, Vince Pangrazio, Robert Salonites, Mark Richardson, Jim Reiss and their families. I always felt at ease with them because they accepted – or at least tolerated – my severely flawed nature.

Early in my career Curt Olsen, Doug Schweitzer and John Baima provided me my first opportunity out of college. Which was nice considering I once hit John over the head with a shovel and used to pummel Mr. Schweitzer and Mr. Olsen in my garage. Current business colleagues Paul Pickle, Steve Litchfield, Mike Sivetts, Rick Goerner, Fabian Battaglia, Roger Holliday, Carmen Isham and the late Lance Robertson, have always been supportive. And of course Jimmy P, who I'm convinced could have made a great mob boss, and Ralph Brandi, the only executive who swears worse than me. Both believed in me enough to give me a shot. All these colleagues were instrumental in not only being patient with my unorthodox business practices but also providing sound advice in how to become a more refined executive. Special thanks to Farhad Mafie for helping me with the cover and Michele Sweeney, the first to provide feedback.

I am appreciative of two-term assemblyman and current Mayor Cameron Smyth not only for his leadership and friendship but tolerance of my profanity-laced outbursts regarding city issues. Deserving of mention is also State Senator Tony Strickland (ret.) and Strong America colleague Morris Thomas.

To my fellow boxing trainers Chico Magana, Larry and Mark Duran, Carlos Campos, Terry Washington and Larry Pope, thanks for your dedication in helping the neighborhood kids improve their boxing skills and showing them a better path. It is heartening to see some of the kids we trained - Juan and David Ruiz, Rudy Martinez, Chencho Chavez, Hector Guizar, Jesus Quinones, Tony Di Nardo -raising their families while excelling in careers.

I owe a debt of gratitude to AIA industry executives, all very accomplished people who over the years have taught me much about industry leadership. Industry executives Tania Hanna, Remy Nathan, Ralph DeNino, Paul Paolozzi were directly helpful in the process and I am extraordinarily appreciative for their efforts.

Louis Ippolito, Sonny D, Bobby Mayo, Johnny Nardone, Tony Palermo, Tommy Fratto, Rudy Fratto – thanks for your trust and support and keeping me out of cement shoes; and a special thanks to Rudy and Tommy for having my back in Chicago! Tribal loyalties are seldom understood. Thanks to good friend the late Johnny Fratto Sr. and his son Johnny Fratto Jr., who successfully transformed in to a capitalist.

Thanks to one-percenters the late Terry "The Tramp" Orendorff, Rusty Coones, Joey Vlad, Dennis Grindeland,

Pastor Phil Aquilar and Dominic Ferrara for the interesting life experiences.

As a young Chicago street kid I never imagined myself partying with the rich and famous. Consequently I would be remiss in not acknowledging the late Hugh Hefner for his graciousness and hospitality by adding me to his guest list at the request of Dr. Mark Saginor, who has always treated me like a son and whom I am fortunate to have as a friend. For years I partied with the "Usual Suspects" Jimmy Van Patten, Dr. Bruce Hensel, Mike Berk, Jim and Sheila Feuchtinger, Ron and Kathy McCabe.

In 2011, after attending my 50th birthday party, Larry Elder convinced me that my life was interesting enough to write a book about it. He told me that over the years he had always believed the stories I told him were "bullshit" – that is until he did the research and met the characters in those stories first-hand. Larry provided the needed inspiration and helped get the project off the ground in its initial phase by not only giving me useful advice and input but introducing me to Tina Marie Ito, my literary agent, who has been indispensable throughout the entire process. Without her efforts, the book would have never become a reality.

Paternal aunts Arlene Damofle, Linda Pacino, Karen Costello and Adele Handler for helping me with some of the Costello family history. My sister Margie, in between arguments, found enough moments of clarity to assist as well. Maternal aunt Carol Kauss helped me gain a better understanding of the mother I knew far too short a time.

My late cousin Iron Mike Ecklund was by far my closest relative. Mike was never exactly a "people person" and had a short fuse that burned fast. I pray he finds the peace in death that eluded him in life. And a nod of the head to other relatives who have passed on – Uncle Paul Andrzejczak,

Larry Costello Jr., Gino Costello, Lisa Van Vorst and Uncle Larry Costello. I must admit this side of the family seems to find the most interesting ways of dying.

Special thanks to the Baio family, especially Scott and Rene, who have been our adopted clan for nearly twenty years.

And most of all, a HUGE thanks to my wife Janell. Truly a wonder woman, she is a loving spouse, mother and successful small-business owner.

August 2017

Los Angeles

Made in the USA
Columbia, SC
07 April 2020